EUROPE BY CAMPERVAN

Turn Your Vanlife Dreams into Roadtrip Reality

Chris Wise

Mandrill Media

Publisher: Mandrill Media
"Treetops", 128 The Mount, York, England. YO24 1AS

Contact: chris.wise@mandrillmedia.tv

Discover more on my campervan blog: Vanlifevirgins.com

Much travelled mugs (on cover) made in Yorkshire by Dialectable.

To the "Hubster" - without whose inspiration, open-mindedness and astounding location research skills, our amazing adventure would still be a dream.

CONTENTS

DISCLAIMER

This book is a general guide to taking an extended road trip through Europe in a campervan or motorhome. Its author and contributors share their personal experiences to help you prepare for your own adventure and issues you may encounter while travelling.

The author, publisher and contributors are not lawyers or motor engineers. The content of this book is not intended to be, and must never be used as, a substitute for professional legal advice or technical advice from a professional camper van or motorhome engineer.

While every effort has been made to include accurate and up-to-date information, the publisher, author and contributors assume no responsibility for any inaccuracies, errors or inconsistencies in the content of this book. Many of the topics covered - including international travel restrictions, laws, rules, regulations, and the availability of camping facilities - are continually changing. The author, publisher and contributors give no warranty about the legality of using any of the camping locations referred to in this book. Readers must refer to the current national laws, local regulations and site-specific permissions at the time of their visit to any country or region.

All trademarks, logos and brand names mentioned in this book are the property of their respective owners. All company, product and service names used in this website are for identification purposes only. Use of these names,trademarks and brands does not imply endorsement.

This book contains links to websites and apps which are owned by third parties. These are included for information and convenience only. The author, publisher and contributors have no control over the operation and content of these websites and organisations and make no warranties about the information contained in them. If you access any third-party websites or apps, you do so entirely at your own risk.

The publisher and author are providing this book and its content on an "as is" basis. Your use of the information in this book is at your own risk, and your use of this book implies your acceptance of this disclaimer.

1. LET'S JUST DO IT

I'm not prone to lightbulb moments, but this was a big one.

I was in our VW campervan, parked in the pouring rain outside our local hospital, waiting to pick up my partner Steve after his shift in the Endoscopy department.

I spotted him through the misted up windscreen. He looked every bit like a man who had spent ten hours doing what they do in endoscopy departments.

He climbed into the passenger seat, pulled the door shut and removed his dripping hood.

"I've just had an idea," I beamed. "Why don't we let out the flat and use the rent to go round Europe in the van. You know, take the gap year we never had?"

"Hmmm," he replied, "let me think about it."

But before I could turn the ignition, he added, "Yes."

And that was that. It was a simple yet monumental idea for folks like us who had both worked continuously since we left school, never taken "sabbaticals," and scarcely imagined backpacking to Margate let alone Machu Pichu.

Sure, we'd both enjoyed family holidays, but nothing even approaching the potential adventure that rooted itself firmly in our imaginations on that miserable autumn day.

Right from the start, our plan was never about disappearing forever or taking up permanent van life. It was about finally taking a big break. It was about switching our lives off and seeing what happened when we switched them on again - about daring to take the big road trip so many people dream about but never manage to pull off.

But could we really do it, for a year, in a campervan?

We'd not had our Vee-dub T6 camper for long. We'd christened him "Ovis" because we reckoned he'd been a bread van before we had him converted.

Ovis had treated us to great weekends in the Yorkshire Dales and a fabulous fortnight in "Devcornwallerset." That's our generic term for the Southwest of England, and an ominous sign that we struggle to know exactly where we are in parts of our own country, let alone the Arctic Circle or Albania - destinations which were now on the cards for our mega trip.

When we told friends and family about our ingenious plan, their instant reaction was always a widening of the eyes. I suspect this was more to do with who had come up with the plan than the plan itself. But it didn't take any of them long to follow up with comments like "Oh, that's something I've always dreamed of doing", or "How fantastic" - followed by an extensive bucket list of European destinations they would love to visit given the chance.

We know we are incredibly lucky to have made our trip of a lifetime. But the reality of driving away from our everyday lives, jobs was not easy. We had major spanners thrown in our works.

Britain leaving the EU restricted our freedom of movement and called for a radical re-thinking of our travel plans several times. On a couple of occasions, it almost made us give up and head home.

The not insignificant matter of a global pandemic piled on pressure and uncertainty about any travel, delaying our departure by at least two years.

Add to the mix parking careers, winding down a business, our twice postponed wedding taking place a month before we left and the tenant for our flat falling through a week before we set off, and you'll get some idea of what we were up against.

Finally, we did set off - though with nothing like a fixed plan. As we drove our camper onto the ferry at Harwich, all we knew for certain was that the first stage of our adventure would take us North, well into the Arctic Circle.

I should explain that before this, our most ambitious adventure had been spending Christmas on a soggy campsite in Weston Super Mare.

So yes, we were unashamedly van life virgins. But we've picked up so much information and top tips on preparing for and surviving a big road trip, I decided to pull it all together in a one-stop shop to help and encourage other newbies - this book.

It's not a detailed list of amazing places we've visited in our camper - that's for later books. This is a general guide - containing all the useful and essential stuff we wish someone had told us before we set off.

It's a combination of practical advice and useful checklists based on our our experiences travelling over 21,000 miles through twenty countries. I hope it ticks off lots of issues and frees up your time and imagination for the exciting job – deciding where to go on *your* adventure.

But more than anything, I hope our experiences give you inspiration and encouragement to make your dream road trip happen.

Trust me, we are the most unlikely people to have done this. And if *we* can make a big van life adventure work – I reckon anyone can.

2. MAKE YOUR BIG TRIP HAPPEN

I'm fully aware that van life adventures don't happen without funds.

Maybe you have savings? We didn't. Perhaps you're ready to blow your pension pot on a long-awaited adventure? We hadn't quite reached that stage. Maybe you've had a windfall or inheritance? We didn't fit into that category either.

I wouldn't presume to recommend how you should fund your foray into van life. All I can do is share how we managed to do it.

After nearly thirty years of paying a mortgage, I'm now lucky enough to own a smart flat at the top of a Georgian terraced house in York, England. Our estate agent described it as a "maisonette." They said it was quirky and suitable for high-end business lets. When they predicted what the monthly rental income might be, our trip took a big leap towards reality. After ploughing money into my home for years, it was payback time.

Three months before we planned to leave, the agents took photos, listed the flat on their website and had an enthusiastic tenant lined up within days. We'd agreed to leave the flat "semi-furnished." In truth, that meant leaving a few items we couldn't squeeze into the attic or my daughter's garden shed, plus several pieces of furniture that, due to the old house being characterfully wonky, were screwed to the walls.

Then disaster. A week before we were due to leave, the tenancy fell through. The ferry was booked. There was no going back. So, I all but gave my 13-year-old Mini to one of those online car-buying companies. It had become pretty unreliable, so no tears were shed. Plus, its sale meant we had some cash to cover our first month on the road while the agent searched for another tenant.

We were also lucky enough to own our campervan, Cliff. (I'll explain our torturous route to settling on Cliff shortly). We'd also paid for our camper's upgrades and insurance before we left. So, when the agent found another tenant within a fortnight, we discovered we'd have £1800 a month – that's £30 per day each – to live on.

I'm a bit wary about mentioning this figure as I don't want to give any guarantee that you will be able to travel for a lengthy period on this daily budget. You may not be able to survive on as many ham and cheese toasties as we did.

Our daily allowance had to cover all our food and drink, diesel and LPG gas, road and ferry tolls, campsite and parking fees, the occasional laundrette, and tickets to must-see attractions.

Choosing some of the most expensive countries in Europe for the first leg of our trip put huge pressure on our budget. One month, we were down to sixty-five pence before the next chunk of rent money arrived. Much later in our adventure, a long stay in cut-price Albania left us with hundreds of pounds in the travel kitty.

In the interest of full disclosure, we did have about £700 up our sleeves thanks to the generosity of guests at our wedding. We decided our nuptial nest egg would only be used to fund special treats, mostly visits to attractions. We blew a substantial chunk of it having Lego robots serve us an amazing meal at Lego House in Denmark. Details of that experience and others on our travels are for later books and YouTube videos on *The Campervan Channel*.

So, what did we discover about setting out to fund our trip in this way?

First, if you have a mortgage on your property, it's possible your bank won't allow you to rent out your home. You'll need to check.

You may be able to let your property for six months, but we were told ours was more likely to attract a tenant if it was available for a year.

I'd strongly recommend placing your home with a professional letting agency which will look after everything while you're away. Apart from it being annoying to get a call about a leaking toilet when you're sunning yourself on the Amalfi Coast – there's absolutely nothing you can do about it. The agents will charge a fee for liaising with your tenants and fixing any problems, but it's worth paying to forget about any minor problems back home.

And remember the obvious, if you do let your property for a year, you have no right to return to it until that year is up - whatever happens on your trip!

GETTING OFF WORK

Even if you can fund your adventure, work commitments may put a big spanner in the works. I was lucky, or unlucky - depending on how you look at it. My business, producing videos for the NHS, had been flat-lining. COVID gave the NHS more important things to think about and, understandably, commissioning videos was not a priority. If ever there was a time to take a break from work - this was it.

By then, Steve was working for a private healthcare company. They were keen not to lose him and agreed an unpaid sabbatical, promising he'd have a job on his return. I appreciate many people won't be this fortunate and must wait until a time in their lives when work commitments are less of a restriction.

The key for us was that no-one was dependent upon us. We were in our fifties - Steve just in, me just about to fall out. We were fit enough to get the best out of a big trip and had simply reached the point in our lives where we both said, "What the hell – let's go for it."

3. CAMPERVAN, MOTORHOME OR CARAVAN?

Clearly no van life adventure is going to happen without a mobile home. At the start of this, we had our much-loved VW camper, but it soon became clear he was not up to the enormity of the trip we now envisaged.

I'll take you through our somewhat chaotic journey to finding the right vehicle. If you don't already have a campervan or motorhome, our floundering should help you make the right choice.

The very idea for our big European trip sprung from our deep love of Ovis.

We first caught the campervan bug hiring campers for weekends away. It wasn't long before we traded in our everyday car for a silver T6 Transporter panel van and had him transformed into the aforementioned Ovis by a specialist converter.

Over time, we lowered his suspension and lavished gifts on him. We added smart decals, VW camper cushions, chrome side bars and a set of stunning five-spoke alloy wheels.

Our short-wheelbase wonder repaid us with some fantastic days by the sea, weekends in the Lake District and Yorkshire Dales, and a couple of week-long wanderings across the UK.

He was perfect - compact enough to sleep two in comfort and fit into a Tesco car park slot. Versatile enough to be our weekend getaway vehicle and our daily drive. A great little van that did lots of jobs brilliantly while managing to make even us appear a little bit cool.

But as our idea for a year-long European grand tour began to crystalise, a horrifying realisation crept up on us. Ovis was not big enough. There was no way we could cram a year's worth of clothes and other essentials into his locker space, plus, he didn't have an onboard loo.

The lack of loo had not bothered me on UK jaunts because we'd always stayed at official campsites with ablution blocks. But there was no chance of such facilities in the depths of Swedish forests or on the tops of Norwegian mountains that were now on our wish list of locations to explore. We had to take a toilet with us.

Hardcore camping folks have no qualms about heading off into the wilderness equipped with nothing but a spade and an old newspaper for their toiletry requirements. I am not and never will be one of those people.

In truth, I'm not at all comfortable with answering the call of nature inside a vehicle – even if it does involve a perfectly adequate onboard loo. It's the thought of driving along with that tank... enough said!

There was another issue. Steve and I had got on perfectly well in the small but brilliantly designed space inside Ovis on short trips. However, spending an entire year in such confinement was highly likely to result in a murder.

The rest of this chapter explains how we eventually ended up with the leisure vehicle that would become our full-time home for over a year. As it turned out, we had plenty of time to make several wrong decisions.

PLANNING AND THE PANDEMIC

We started serious planning for our trip during the first wave of COVID.

In those early days, country after country closed their borders. Waves of infections shut down entire cities. There was no way we could set a departure date with confidence, let alone plan any kind of route.

And although I appreciate this is very small beer compared to the tragic consequences the pandemic had on many people's lives, COVID did cause havoc in the leisure vehicle industry.

Across the world, factories shut their doors and sent staff home. Campervan and motorhome production lines stopped for lengthy periods. When they did re-start, COVID-safe working practices made them slow. Leisure vehicles were soon in short supply.

Manufacturers struggled to meet back orders. Components became unobtainable. Then, on top of everything, there was a global shortage of the crucial computer chips that feature in the electronic systems of all modern vehicles. Soon, camper and motorhome builders couldn't source base vans and chassis - the building blocks for their creations.

It grew into a perfect storm. Dealers couldn't supply and because of the on-going restrictions on foreign travel, staycations boomed and the demand for camping vehicles in the UK was higher than ever.

Selfishly, the chaos in the mobile home market ended up working in our favour. Prices held while we blundered from one type of vehicle to another trying to find the right one.

AU REVOIR OVIS

You've probably gathered that we adored Ovis. The prospect of getting rid of him was horrific and we really wanted to stick with the VW brand. We considered conversions of longer wheelbase Volkswagen Transporters which would have given us an extra forty centimetres of van, but they still weren't big enough.

We managed to find some rare Vee-dub campers that had a built-in toilet. These had their pop-top roof hinged at the front, creating enough roof height at the back to accommodate a shower and loo.

We drooled at top-of-the-range Westfalia conversions with this configuration. They were the smart, competent vans you'd expect from the German company that first converted VW campers back in the fifties. But they were way beyond our budget and that clever toilet felt a little too close to the kitchen for our comfort.

How about taking a toilet tent with us, with a so-called porta-potty? No. Horrible idea. And besides, we had no space to store either a tent or a giant plastic potty. Thankfully.

In an ideal world, we would have wandered into a VW or campervan dealer and bought a humungous Volkswagen Grand California. I'd had a sneak preview of Volkswagen's conversions of its larger Crafter van while filming for *The Campervan Channel* on You Tube. They have fixed beds, a shower in a wet room and the coolest of light-coloured interiors that look like an airline cabin. They are stunning and, of course, have legendary VW build quality throughout.

The only un-lovable thing about them is their price. Brand new, Grand Cali's start at around £80,000 region. Specialist Crafter conversions can cost even more.

Then, unexpectedly, a brainwave. We could keep Ovis if we persuaded him to tow a small, two-berth caravan. After scouting around caravan dealerships, we saw a funky looking Bailey D2-2 and bought it, brand new, for about £17,000.

CARAVAN CAPERS

In the past, if someone had told me I would one day buy a caravan, I would have declared them insane. But Bailey, as we called him, didn't look like most of the white boxes on wheels I can't summon up an emotional response to. He was a cool grey, with curved rear corners that made him look more like a cute little horsebox than a caravan.

We had a towbar fitted to Ovis, hooked Bailey up and hauled him away on a few weekend camping expeditions and what turned out to be a very decisive trip to Devcornwallerset.

We hated it. Bailey's accommodation was impressive. Remarkably comfortable, with a great heating and hot water system, a sizeable oven and the roomiest of corner showers. Devcornwallerset wasn't the issue; it was as beautiful as ever. What depressed us was towing and manoeuvring our otherwise great little caravan. I have always adored driving, but dragging Bailey behind us transformed it into a chore.

Caravan speed restrictions weren't the problem. I wouldn't dare tow the thing any faster than the 60mph motorway limit. The devastating impact on Ovis's fuel consumption would also have been forgiven if everything else had stacked up.

Even the nightmare (for us novices) of reversing Bailey into a tiny pitch on a campsite might have become less of a challenge with practise. Hats off to true caravanners who manage to tow and manoeuvre massive trailers.

Perhaps we had become accustomed to arriving at a campsite in Ovis, popping his roof, switching on the gas and being up and running in what felt like thirty seconds. For us, the palaver of caravanning; all that hitching, towing, worrying about weight, parking, levelling, and managing *two* vehicles instead of one was just too much faff.

After owning Bailey for just seven weeks, we put him up for sale and, due to COVID reducing caravan stocks too, sold him within 24 hours, for a little less than we'd paid for him.

I must report that much later, during our travels, we saw plenty of evidence that confident and competent caravanners *can* tow their homes on wheels to some extraordinary and seemingly inaccessible places. Though if you're thinking about informal camping – going a bit off grid – I think it's fair to say it would be pretty much impossible with a caravan. Later chapters will explain this more fully when we look at where you can overnight for no or little cost in Europe and the UK.

Maybe we would have mastered caravanning, eventually, but for us, it just felt wrong. We'd learned some big lessons with no major impact on our wallets.

So, we went in search of a compromise. Something with the space, comfort, and facilities of our ill-fated caravan in a self-contained, smaller, and reasonably priced unit. After much internet research, we settled on a small, coach-built motorhome.

A MOMENTARY MOTORHOME

At that point, we truly believed the answer to all our problems was an Auto-trail F-Line F60, coach-built motorhome on the latest Ford Transit chassis. At about six metres long, it wasn't (that) much longer than Ovis, but having its living space in a wider motorhome body instead of being squeezed inside a van, it managed to include a washroom and an impressive kitchen. The only drawback – no fixed bed.

Finding an actual F60 was also tricky – particularly one with the automatic gearbox we wanted. Those COVID-induced supply problems and huge customer demand meant dealers couldn't guarantee delivery dates on new vehicles.

We eventually came across an auto F60 on a dealer's forecourt in Somerset. With the caravan proceeds in our pocket, we put down a deposit and knew the sale of Ovis (cue gut-wrenching sob) would eventually make up the difference. A couple of weeks later, we picked up "Harrison." You've guessed – Harrison (the) Ford.

And here's my first big top tip that's the result of painful experience. If you are buying any new or used campervan or motorhome from a dealership, do everything humanly possible to buy from a dealer that is physically close to you. We've bought new vehicles from dealers many miles from our home twice, and both times lived to regret it.

In our experience, anything from minor snagging problems to major component replacements are surprisingly par for the course when you buy a leisure vehicle which has been mostly built by hand.

A dealer who sells you a vehicle *will* put things right – but for us, a 400-mile round trip to have the heating system replaced on Harrison after only a week of ownership would have been a complete pain.

So, we ended up taking him back to his factory birthplace on the outskirts of Grimsby because it was closer. The manufacturer happily replaced the boiler. But because of COVID social distancing, Steve couldn't wait inside for the work to be done and spent the day loitering around an industrial estate that smelt of fish.

Later, when a couple of pieces of internal trim started peeling off Harrison, it was less hassle to just glue them back on ourselves.

But by far the biggest disappointment, for us, was the way our little motorhome rattled. I appreciate that coach-built motorhomes are a lightweight box fastened to a vehicle chassis and cab. I also understand that the living accommodation needs to be as light as possible to keep most campers or motorhomes under 3.5 tonnes. It's the weight most folks are entitled to drive on their driving licences.

(More on that later too).

But I was not prepared for the amount of rattling, squeaking, and creaking that came from the living quarters when we drove along. I'm not talking about the inevitable jangling from crockery, storage containers, bottles, and food tins. I mean noises from the bodywork and fittings - the clicks and rattles from plastic blinds, flyscreens, and skylights as the vehicle flexes or goes over the slightest bumps.

We stuck cushioning pads on anything we thought was the source of a creak. We used cable ties to tighten the metal stays on the windows which rattled. But it wasn't enough. After the most unpleasant drive home from a weekend in the Yorkshire Dales, we were deaf, angry and had had enough.

Maybe we'd been spoilt by the solid build of our converted Vee-Dub Transporter. Maybe most folks offset flimsiness and the odd rattle against the extra comfort, sophistication, and space these vehicles provide. Maybe top end motorhomes don't make the noises our entry-level one did. We couldn't know - this was the first and only motorhome we'd owned.

What we knew for certain was that we could not contemplate spending an entire year in that space, so Harrison had to go. We sold him to a couple of experienced motor-homers upgrading to a more modern vehicle. After a thorough test drive, they were perfectly happy with the way Harrison performed. Maybe our newbie expectations were unrealistic?

Luckily, the continuing COVID-induced shortages and high demand for leisure vehicles meant we didn't lose too much money on our short foray into coach-built motor-homing. Our search resumed for the perfect getaway vehicle.

CLIFF RESCUE

By now, we were clearer about what we wanted. It had to be a van conversion. We assumed it would be more rigid than a coach-built motorhome.

Second, it had to be around six metres long. Anything smaller would not have had significantly more space than the Vee-dub. Anything bigger would limit where we could park.

It needed a fixed bed because we couldn't face dismantling sofas every night for twelve months and have an onboard toilet and shower to give us off-grid freedom.

Having viewed many new and used campervans, we were determined to avoid the beige and chintzy variety. Some we snooped around had all the ambience of a mobile care home. We wanted a minimalist, clean, simple interior with no frills.

After weeks of online searching and YouTube viewing (mostly by ace internet researcher Steve), we settled on a Sunlight Cliff 600 Adventure, and came up against the familiar issue of not being able to find one in the flesh.

Sunlight is one of several camper and motorhome brands in the German Erwin Hymer group. Marketing for their campervans targets younger, sporty, surfer-types. To say that neither Steve nor I fit into that demographic is something of an understatement, but we like to think we're young in spirit and we both liked the simple, smart designs, practical layout, and cool colours of Sunlight's campers.

Sunlights are common in Europe, but not so in the UK, so our best bet for seeing examples was at one of Sunlight's few UK dealers. Our nearest dealer, in Yorkshire, had just sold their last Cliff 600 and had couldn't confirm when they'd get another.

So, we made the 200-mile trip to Goodmans Motorhomes at Waltham Abbey in Essex. They hire out a fleet of Sunlight campers and motorhomes during the summer and sell some of them off in the Autumn. (Incidentally, hiring a camper or motorhome is an incredibly useful experience if you're a newbie or want to test out a specific kind of van before you buy.)

We walked into the yard at Goodmans, and there he was. *Just* what we were looking for. He was in cool campovolo grey, and the icing on the cake - he was an automatic. Steve's intensive research had revealed no sign of this actual van.

"Oh, it's just come in," the manager told us. "It's not for the hire fleet, it's for sale."

Within half an hour, the deal was done, and the deposit paid.

Clearly, our route to finding the right vehicle was a haphazard one, and our wrong choices would have cost us dearly if we had been messing things up in more normal times.

So, to help you avoid our mistakes, the next chapter is a more practical checklist of features you might consider when you're narrowing down the right camper or motorhome for you.

4. CHOOSING YOUR HOME ON WHEELS – CHECKLIST

We've met folks exploring Europe in everything from sparkling new, American-style, luxury motorhomes to tiny 1950s caravans that looked as if they'd fall apart before they reached the end of the street, let alone scaled the Albanian Alps.

We've also encountered talented souls who've transformed retired ambulances or monstrous ex-army trucks into the most amazing, bespoke mobile homes. We even met a pioneering young couple tackling a nine-month trip in an all-electric campervan.

Our distinct lack of DIY skills meant a self-build camper was never on the cards, so like most folks, we had to choose from the overwhelming range of new and used, conventional motorhomes and campervans on the market.

Before I tell you more about the camper we finally settled on - and the reasons we chose him - let's zoom right out to the big picture and look at the broad options newbie van-lifers face when they're right at the start of their search for a home on wheels.

BASE VEHICLES

Despite the enormous choice in the styles of campervan and motorhomes, there's a high probability you'll end up with one built on a Fiat Ducato.

When we started our search, three out of four campers sold in Europe are based on this Italian light commercial vehicle that's been around since 1981. According to Fiat, over half a million mobile homes have Fiat mechanicals. I thought it would have been more.

There are good reasons for this popularity. Ducato vans offer class-leading space for their length and motor home converters are involved in the design of special camper versions of the Ducato chassis.

There's another reason motorhomes and campers can look a bit samey. Those based on Peugeot Boxer and Citroen Jumper vans are dead ringers for Fiats. It's a case of same bodies and chassis – different engines. The three motoring marques are all in the giant PSA automotive group, so all this carbon-copying is above board and amicable.

There are many variations in wheelbases, lengths, and heights of all these vehicles. This allows camper and motorhome manufacturers to offer a huge choice when it comes to the dimensions of their mobile homes and what goes inside them.

Predictably, our "Cliff" is based on a Fiat Ducato. But the Italian brand wouldn't have been my first choice.

I blame my dad. He was a motor mechanic for most of his working life and would turn in his grave if he knew I'd bought anything with a Fiat badge on it. He passionately believed in the old cliche that Fiat stood for Fix It Again Tomorrow. In fairness, Dad's prejudice was based on fixing Fiat cars that rusted away before his eyes back in the 1970s and 80s - not today's modern motorhomes.

I should mention that commercial vehicles like the Mercedes Sprinter and the Ford Transit also provide the basic van bodies and chassis for an increasing number of perfectly competent campervans and motorhomes.

BODY STYLE OPTIONS

If you're looking for a self-propelled leisure vehicle (i.e., not a caravan) there are three basic body styles to choose from.

First, there are **campervans**. Converters create a camper's living space within the skin of what would otherwise be a standard delivery van. The kind of thing that delivers your Amazon parcels.

The second choice is a **coach built or "low profile" motorhome**. Manufacturers create these by sticking a purpose-built accommodation box onto a light commercial vehicle chassis. The accommodation unit often has a bit that sticks out over the vehicle cab, providing extra room for storage or a small bed.

The third possibility is an **"A-class" style motorhome**. These are the larger, boxy-shaped motorhomes that can look as though they've come out of the design department at Playmobil. With this type of motorhome, there's no trace of an original cab. The entire body is built on either a van chassis, or in the case of mahoosive motorhomes, on the chassis from a truck.

A-class motorhomes are often big, luxurious, and expensive. If they weigh over seven tonnes, it's likely you'll have to pass an additional driving test to drive one. More on licences and vehicle weight classifications later. Bet you can't wait!

HOW WILL YOU USE YOURS?

Even when you've chosen which of the three main types of mobile home suits you and your budget, finding an actual vehicle can be a bewildering process.

From our experiences – and you've seen how we struggled to decide on even the type of mobile home we wanted - my top tip would be to show iron will and think carefully about how you intend to use your camper or motorhome.

List which features you consider essential *before* you look at any actual vehicles. Otherwise, you're guaranteed to fall in love at first sight and could end up with something that's impractical for you.

We've discovered that living in a van or motorhome is not always plain sailing. If your van doesn't meet your specific needs, it could irritate you throughout your adventure.

We spent months peering into campervans, sussing out accessories and different layouts. We watched online videos, visited dealerships, and even spent a mind-boggling day at a motorhome and campervan exhibition at the NEC. It's an intensive experience, but a terrific way to inspect what's on the market.

Unfortunately, we *didn't* start our search with a clear checklist. If we had, we could have avoided buying two vehicles that didn't work out for us.

I'm going to share the checklist we now know we should have had, to help you build your own wish list.

SIZE MATTERS

Our Cliff's accommodation is inside the dimensions of a regular 5.99 metre Fiat Ducato van. He's too long to park in a standard car parking space, but we usually manage to squeeze him in somewhere if we can find a space that allows for a bit of an overhang.

Six metres seems to be a watershed in camper lengths. Anything longer, like the 6.4 metre version of our van, will be harder to park and incur higher charges on ferries and for pitches at some campsites. A lorry driver I met on a campsite recently was hiring different sized motorhomes before deciding which one to buy. He found the rear overhang on longer vehicles difficult to manage - and this was a man who drove articulated trucks for a living!

The shorter 5.4 metre version of our van is more car park friendly. We considered one of these as it would have been easier to manage and still given us the fixed bed we were looking for. However, the extra space would not have been significantly more than that in our beloved VW T6 camper – certainly not enough to justify the intense grief we went through in parting with our Vee-dub. So, like many folks, we went for the middle-of-the road six metre van.

Most campervan and motorhome manufacturers offer models around these three basic lengths. The length you choose has an enormous impact on what space and features you can have inside. There's much more variation in lengths with motorhomes.

BED OPTIONS

When it comes to choosing any camper or motorhome, a key priority is deciding how many people will sleep in it. Also consider whether you can tolerate converting sofas into a bed every night or whether you need a permanent, fixed bed.

Our Cliff has a fixed, effectively king-sized bed at the back. I say "fixed" bed. Technically, the bed will split and fold up against the sides of the van to open up storage space for bikes. But we have no need of that and can leave the bed in place permanently. A godsend.

Our bed feels massive. As a six-foot-two individual, my feet do catch on the window blinds. A smaller window set higher in the van wall would be better for lanky folks like me. However, I cannot fault the comfort of the bed and am genuinely surprised how well I sleep in the van.

We sleep transversely – i.e., across the van. Our heads are against one solid side wall and our feet against the window opposite. Longer 6.4 metre vans tend to have more bed space and may allow you to slumber "in-line" with the van – with your head against the back doors and your feet pointing towards the windscreen.

In Cliff, we also have the option to drop the table in the "dinette" area and use the tabletop and small mattress that was supplied with the van to create an extra single bed up front. But we don't need to accommodate three, so we've saved space and weight by leaving the bed board and mattress at home.

Manufacturers offer many other sleeping solutions. Some campervans have rear lounges whose sofas convert into beds at night. Too much faff for us. Other vans, like the "601" version of Cliff, have two double bunk beds that will accommodate four adults.

And since we bought Cliff, increasing numbers of camper manufacturers now install pop-top roofs. These ingenious, hinged lids on the roof open to create an extra bedroom. You climb "upstairs" using a ladder. They've been a hallmark of small VW campers since the beginning of time, and it's a bit of mystery to me why other manufacturers have taken so long to catch on.

Motorhomes sometimes squeeze additional beds in a carbuncle above the cab. These tend to be for smaller humans.

Other motorhomes have coach-built bodies that are high enough to accommodate a double bed that can be stored in the ceiling and winched down when you're ready to hit the sack. That's easier than assembling a bed from bits of your sofa.

Beds are clearly a vital element of any home on wheels. The options above are only a taster of the inventive solutions converters come up with. Just decide what your sleeping requirements are likely to be and whether any van you look at can deliver them.

HEATING

As I'm writing this chapter, we're living in our van, in the UK, in December. My Mum is expecting to receive a call anytime telling her that we've both died from hypothermia. Newsflash Mother! We are toasty warm inside our van and have boiling hot water on tap. (Well, on two small taps.)

Campervan or motorhome manufactures tend to install heaters made by a handful of specialist companies.

Cliff has a Truma Combi 6 heater. It's one of the most impressive accessories on our van, running on either gas or electric, or a mix of both. Experience so far suggests everything gets hotter, quicker when gas is involved.

The control panel is easy to use once you get the hang of it. Set the ambient temperature you want and warm air flows into the living space through five heating vents dotted around the van.

We can set hot water to eco or hot. There's even a boost setting if we're in a rush to have a shower or wash the dishes.

The heating controls *can* throw up the odd error code. In our experience, these are usually due to user error. Either we've set the heater to run on gas and not switched the gas supply on; or we've told the heater to use mains power when we're not connected to an electric hook-up.

Occasionally the system has over heated and shut itself down - usually because we've accidentally blocked one of the air vents near the boiler. So far, a few deep breaths, a cooling off period and a reset have always solved the problem.

Whale is another popular brand for camper and caravan heaters. Just make sure your dealer or previous owner demonstrates how to use these systems, and check that they work. They're not the most exciting device to consider when you're looking for a camper or mobile home, but they are one of the most essential for supporting van life as we know it.

TOILET

I'd prefer not to talk toilets, but it's undeniable that having a loo on board your mobile home gives you freedom. Freedom *not* to go staggering across a campsite to the toilet block in the dead of night to answer the call of nature. Freedom to camp away from official campsites (where you're allowed to), providing you can return to civilisation to empty toilet waste on a regular basis.

For the uninitiated, many larger campers and motorhomes have a toilet that looks like the loo you have at home. The main difference is that it flushes into a sealed, plastic box, politely referred to in camper land as a "cassette." You need to add special potions into the cassette to combat odours and break down its contents into... well, you'll know when you have the misfortune to encounter it.

Ever so often, you'll need to empty your cassette. How often depends on a range of factors too delicate to discuss. You're likely to have a "full" indicator in your loo. When the time comes, you open a trapdoor on the outside side of your van, slide out the sealed cassette and trundle it off to a special place.

Many campsites have designated places to empty your toilet waste or "black" waste as it's ominously called. These disposal points are known as chemical waste points, latrines or Elsan toilets. We, however, now use the more descriptive term we saw on one of these facilities at a Dutch campsite - "Loosplatts."

Europe also introduced us to machines that conduct the entire loosplatting process automatically - discreetly emptying, cleaning, and adding chemicals to the cassette behind a closed roller door. Worth two euros of anyone's life savings.

One of these machines I used at a German campsite played me a video while I was waiting for the magic to happen. The video asked if I'd considering becoming a vegetarian? I can't pin down why I found that so disturbing.

Much as I still find the whole concept unpleasant, I've accepted that an onboard loo is unavoidable on our type of trip. As with heaters, camper loos are usually made by one or two major manufacturers and all the magic potions you need to keep them performing sweetly are readily available in camping shops or online.

WASHROOM/ SHOWER

Our loo is in a separate washroom that includes a sink, mirror, shelves, and storage cupboards. The sink has a single mixer tap that we can pull out on a metal hose and insert into a wall bracket, turning it into a shower head. The base of the room is a shower tray with a drain. All very clever and compact.

When we shower, we're supposed to use a shower curtain which hangs from a rail on the ceiling. Given my personal dimensions and the general lack of space, once I'm wet, the curtain clings to me. It's like trying to do your ablutions while you're vacuum packed. Obviously, the bigger your van, the more shower space you'll have to play with. A true wet room won't have a shower curtain to wrestle with.

According to the marketing bumph for our van, hardy types will stick the shower head through the toilet window and take a shower outside. There will never be a time when the world is ready for us doing that.

KITCHEN

There appears to be as many types of kitchens as there are vans. Motorhomes tend to have better equipped galleys because they have more space.

With campers, you play the kitchen compromise game. If you can get away with a simple two-ring gas burner, sink and electric fridge like we do, you'll have more space for storage. Insist on an oven and microwave as well as a hob, and you'll either lose space for something else, or need a bigger van.

Let's just say we survive a prolonged period of van-life with just the two gas burners and our 90-litre fridge which has a small freezer compartment. We may consume too many sandwiches, tinned products, and pasta meals, but haven't starved yet. It's a case of heating things up rather than cooking fancy meals.

With no oven, we can't bake or grill. But here's another top tip. If your van is oven-less, get yourself a *RidgeMonkey*. It's so simple and inexpensive - a kind of hinged sandwich toaster that heats up on your gas ring instead of plugging into an electric supply. It makes superb toasties and can even turn bread into reasonable toast. Thoroughly recommended.

We also have a portable charcoal-fuelled barbeque with an optional pizza stone which also does a wonderful job. It provides an opportunity to "cook," if the weather is good enough to go outside and you're permitted to use a barbie.

Having inspected many campers, we weren't keen on kitchens that included a floor-to-ceiling kitchen unit with a high-level fridge. These tend to be opposite the washroom, cutting the living space in two and making the centre of the van feel quite pinched and claustrophobic. Our fridge is below the worktop, giving the van a more open feel. But it's all down to personal taste.

DINING AREA

As in many campers, Cliff has a "dinette" area. This consists of a double bench seat, with seatbelts and ISOFIX, behind a small table. Passengers can sit in these while you're travelling.

The table has an extension that pivots out creating a surface big enough for four diners. Two diners sit on the bench seat; two more sit on the driver and passenger chairs that are swivelled 180 degrees to face the table.

Other campervans might have removable dining tables in the centre of a rear lounge. At night, these tabletops become part of a bed.

Individual campervan and motorhome converters produce their own solutions to the age-old challenge of cramming as much useful equipment into what is, after all, a small space.

It's impossible to list all the design options here, but when you look at a leisure vehicle, have a serious think about how it will work for you.

5. SURVIVAL GADGETS & GIZMOS

There's no harm in adding widescreen TVs, twinkling awning lights, bike racks or gold-plated taps to your camper or motorhome. After all, van life is about self-expression. But this chapter is about more essential accessories.

After delays and uncertainties caused by COVID, we finally plucked up the courage to commit to a departure date for our big trip. Our ferry crossing from Harwich to the Hook of Holland was inked in for July 1st, 2022.

As D-day approached, and the enormity of living for a year in a campervan really began to hit home, we realised that our new, off-the-shelf vehicle was missing some crucial pieces of kit.

COOKING WITH GAS – UK

Originally, our Cliff was fitted with a single propane gas cannister - one of those familiar orange tanks that supply gas for cooking and heating in campers, motorhomes and caravans in the UK. The blue tanks you may have spotted do the same job but with butane gas.

Camping gas in the UK works on a kind of swapsies system. If a *Calor*-type gas cannister is not already supplied with your campervan or motorhome, you take out an agreement with a gas company and pay for your first cannister and the gas inside it. Thereafter, each time your gas runs out, you swap the empty cannister for a full one at outlets dotted around the country, but only pay for the gas.

Eventually, you will get money back on your last cannister when you no longer need it.

That's all hunky dory - until you run out of gas in Europe.

RE-FILLABLE GAS SYSTEMS – FOR EUROPE

Annoyingly, you can't exchange a UK gas bottle for a European one. This is because each European country has its own unique design of gas cannister, regulator and connector.

The French go a stage further. They have several different types of gas bottles - none of them compatible with the UK version.

So, to make any swappable european cannister fit a UK camper or motorhome, you'll need to buy a country specific adapter/connector, usually from a large supermarket, camping shop or DIY store.

You'll also need to sign up to that country's swapsie system, probably having to provide a retailer with a local address. Some folks get away with their campsite address, apparently.

Then you'll have to pay a deposit on your first bottle in each country and probably be stuck with your old, empty, heavy, bulky bottle. It's no use to a European gas retailer, so they're unlikely to take it off your hands.

All this palaver might be worth enduring if your'e visiting one or two countries for a lengthy period, but we had twenty countries in our travel plans. Thankfully, we came up with an alternative before we left the UK.

RE-FILLABLE GAS SYSTEMS

We decided to have a re-fillable LPG (Liquid Petroleum Gas) system installed in Cliff.

This involves removing the original swappable gas cannister, and replacing it with one or two re-fillable LPG cylinders. These become permanent fixtures in your van - just like its petrol or diesel tank.

We chose a dual *GasLow* LPG system. It took professional engineers half a day to install two, 11kg, yellow tanks, the necessary pipework and safety valves. They also had to cut a hole in Cliff's side (ouch!) for an external filler point and cap. It cost around £650 + VAT.

When the tanks are empty, you re-fill them using the LPG equivalent of a petrol pump, usually at a roadside filling station.

Not every UK forecourt has LPG - and one major retailer has said it's pulling out of providing LPG altogether because it's no longer viable. But you can still find LPG stations - particularly if you use an app like Mylpg.eu.

Crucially for us, LPG is much more common across Europe. We had no problems finding KPG stations in all of the countries we travelled through.

RE-FILLING WITH LPG

The process of re-filling LPG is a bit like adding fuel to your car — though a little more nerve-wracking at first.

The LPG nozzle on the pump must make an air-tight connection with your camper's gas tank. As you clamp it on to the connector on the side of your van, it lets out an alarming, loud whoosh of gas.

Once the connection is sealed, you need to squeeze the dispensing trigger - just like when you're using a petrol pump. The trigger will either clip open or you'll need to keep squeezing it. You may also need to use another finger to press a button on the pump to keep the gas flowing. We find it much easier when it's a two-person job — especially if one of us is trying to decipher instructions on the pump in Norwegian.

Key things we've learned about re-filling LPG are:

* The valve or tap on your onboard gas tank should be turned *off* when you re-fill. It does not need to be *on* to let the gas in.

* Don't worry about over-filling your gas tank. LPG pumps stop dispensing when your tank(s) are about 80 per cent full. So, it's normal for a gauge to never display completely full. I understand this headroom is to allow for any expansion in the gas with changes of temperature. But don't quote me, I have no gas-related qualifications whatsoever.

* If you have two tanks, like we have, a single gauge shows what's left in both tanks. It doesn't show one cannister emptying and then switch to the other. What you see is what you've got... in total.

* When the pump has slowed down and eventually stopped itself, you release the nozzle. Again, it's accompanied by a whoosh of gas. Slightly alarming, but normal.

EUROPEAN LPG ADAPTERS

If you have *GasLo* or any other re-fillable LPG system fitted, make sure your supplier gives you a set of adapters for European countries. We have three which covered all the countries we visited.

There are two further advantages with using LPG in Europe - where it's also referred to as GPL. European LPG is a mix of gases, blended to suit local conditions. If you're filling up in winter, by a frozen Fjord in Norway, your gas will have been blended to freeze at a much lower temperature than LPG that's dispensed in summer on the Cote D'Azur. Clever that.

Even more impressive, re-filling with LPG is much cheaper than swapping portable gas cannisters – in the UK and overseas. Filling both our 11kg tanks from almost empty, at an Asda filling station in the UK cost around £9. Abroad, it's usually cost us around £12 to £15. In Albania, a bargain basement £6.

Long term, savings in gas costs should offset the installation costs of your LPG system, especially on a long trip.

Only Italy caused us a few LPG challenges. The exceptionally safety-conscious Italians don't trust you to re-fill your own LPG and always insist a forecourt attend does it for you.

That may be quaint and slightly irritating during most of the week, but it can become a real pain on Sundays when Italian forecourt attendants take a day off. You can serve yourself petrol or diesel on the Sabbath, but the LPG pump will be switched off because there's no-one around to serve you. Big lesson - don't run out of LPG in Italy on a Sunday like we did.

I should also mention that one weekday attendant at an Italian motorway service station refused point blank to fill our LPG tanks. He said putting gas in vehicles for cooking and heating (as opposed to powering the vehicle engine) was not allowed "anywhere in Italy". Or at least I think that's what he said.

If there is such a law, most Italian forecourts either don't know about it or ignore it. We drove on to the next filling station where an attendant was happy to top up our LPG while cheerily telling us how much he disliked Fiats.

So you *will* find somewhere to re-fill in Italy, but just be aware some fuel stations may refuse.

LEISURE BATTERIES

On most campers and motorhomes, gas fuels the burners on your hob, a grill or oven if you have one, the warm air and water heating, and crazy though it sounds, a gas-powered fridge if you happen to have one.

But you obviously need a supply of electricity too, for the camper's lighting, the USB sockets in the accommodation area, the water pumps that feed your taps and shower, and items like 12-volt TVs.

Twelve-volt power comes from a leisure battery or "house" battery squirrelled away somewhere in your vehicle. This is *not* the familiar battery under your vehicle's bonnet that starts the engine. It's an extra one that's dedicated to running your camping equipment.

There are several ways to keep your leisure battery fully charged. First, just drive. When the alternator – the mini generator that's attached to your engine - has charged the car battery to a sufficient level, it's likely any excess charge will then be diverted to your leisure battery. All this magic is left in the capable hands of a controller installed when a motorhome is built, or a camper converted.

Second, if you plug into a 230-volt mains hook-up at a campsite, that supply will be stepped down to 12-volt to run all your camping appliances and charge up your leisure battery.

Hooking up to mains at a campsite brings any domestic-style 13-amp plug sockets in your camper or motorhome to life – with a full 230-volts. This allows you to run essential domestic appliances such as hair straighteners. However, these sockets do not work, at all, when you're running off your leisure battery alone. (Unless you have an inverter – see below).

Also be aware that campsite power supplies may not be powerful enough to run power-hungry gadgets or several mains gadgets at once. Overloading could trip the campsite supply. At one Italian campsite, the power was so pathetic, just plugging my laptop into the 13-amp socket tripped the circuit. That was an exception though.

But what if you're planning to go a bit off grid? How do you get power when there's no mains and you're hoping to settle in one spot for a few days? We realised we needed a solar panel.

SOLAR PANEL POWER

We had a solar system fitted professionally. A single black panel went on the roof and a solar controller unit went under the driver's seat. The controller is linked to a handy app on our phones that gives us live read-outs of when, where, and how much sun-generated power is flowing.

After some irritating teething problems (the system kept blowing fuses) we had a different type of controller fitted which seemed to sort the problem.

Originally, Cliff was supplied with a 95 Amp Hour (Ah), traditional gel leisure battery. We'd heard that new Lithium-ion batteries, although more costly, would charge quicker, supply around twice as much power as an equivalent sized gel battery, have a long guarantee, and probably pay for themselves… eventually.

As we knew we'd potentially be off grid for weeks, we had a Lithium leisure battery installed and have never looked back. Our year-long trip included many periods away from official campsites and our leisure battery never fell below 75% charge.

It stood up remarkably well during our enforced stay in the UK during the dull, dark days of winter too. Gawd knows how it charged up on days we barely saw the sun. But it did.

The system has been brilliant. We simply don't worry about it. However – another top tip - if you're going to make any changes to your power systems before a big trip, do it as early as you can. They are complicated setups, often involving components from several different manufacturers. Allow time to assess that they all work together and solve any problems before you are forced to depend on them.

The only real power problem I had was with my laptop. It's beefy, and when it's running energy-swallowing video editing software, flattens its own battery in the tap of a mouse pad. It needs full-fat mains to re-charge – but we were hardly ever on campsites. The solution appeared to be an inverter.

INVERTER – MAINS POWER FROM A BATTERY

Here's a non-electrician's explanation of what an inverter does. It's magic.

The 12-volt charge from your leisure battery is fine for powering the 12-volt camping accessories built into your van, but not powerful enough to run the kind of devices that you'd plug into your 13-amp sockets at home.

So, if a slow cooker, microwave, or fondue set is essential on your travels, you could consider having an inverter fitted.

These clever boxes of electronics take 12-volt power from your leisure battery and boost up its voltage so you can run some domestic gadgets. You can either plug a device directly into the three-pin socket on the inverter or have the device's output wired into any 13-amp sockets in your vehicle.

Another warning! There are some quite complicated mathematics involved in working out your power needs and making sure you get an inverter that's big enough to supply that amount of power safely.

I was so frustrated with my laptop dying that I bought a 700W inverter on a visit to camping supplier in Norway, thinking I could fit it while we were on the road. But I bottled out, partly because I didn't have the right tools, but mostly because I feared wrecking our electrical system that was working perfectly and we were relying on so heavily.

During our enforced return to the UK (more on that later) our favourite converter, Colin, at 8Ball Campervan Conversions, fitted the inverter I'd bought.

He also installed a second lithium battery because it turns out inverters are not magic after all. The payback for increasing voltage from your leisure battery is that the battery will run down more quickly. Two batteries – storing 240 Amp hours when full – gave us more capacity.

Unless you're a competent electrician, I'd recommend always going to a qualified campervan or motorhome engineer to work out your exact power requirements, get hold of the right inverter for your needs, and have it fitted. Inverters can generate a lot of power. They require thick cabling and the correct fuses to make sure they're safe and don't cause any damage to your leisure batteries or the rest of your vital electrical systems.

WI-FI BOOSTER

You might argue that having dependable wi-fi in your campervan shouldn't be in a chapter about survival gadgets. I disagree. Without access to news, films, TV, banks, and various apps developed specially for camping, we could easily die.

Even before we left the UK, it was clear from our test runs in the van that we had two challenges when it came to having decent data connections.

First, we love remote "away from it all" camping locations – but almost by definition, they're miles from a decent mobile signal.

Second, when we were on a campsite that claimed to provide its own Wi-Fi network, the signal often ran at speeds that would have frustrated folks in the Stone Age. Pitches some distance from the wi-fi source may have no signal at all. Or, if we did enjoy fast-flowing data during the day, it was guaranteed to dwindle away to a trickle when everyone else on the site finished their tea and logged into BBC I-player to watch Eastenders.

Our local camper and motorhome repair company recommended and installed a wi-fi booster.

Our gadget has two elements. First there's a wi-fi router and signal booster which goes inside your van. It's a mini version of the router you may have at home. It needs an active data SIM card in it to work.

The second part is an external aerial that goes outside on the roof of the van. The two parts are linked by a cable threaded through a hole drilled in the roof.

Top Tip! Make sure whoever installs yours puts tons of sealant around the hole in the roof. Our overhead locker filled with rainwater when we were hit by our first major storm in Sweden. One visit to a Willys supermarket (seriously!) and a tube of sealant later, I managed to fix it.

So how does the booster system work? Here's a non-expert explanation.

BOOSTING YOUR MOBILE SIGNAL

Normally, your mobile phone picks up its signal using a tiny aerial buried inside it. It may struggle in remote areas with weak coverage and labour even more when you are inside a big, signal-blocking metal box like your campervan.

A bigger aerial outside the box is more likely to pick up whatever mobile signal is around. Our device captures that signal, amplifies it, and sends it inside the van to the router.

The router then uses the mobile data stream to create a wi-fi hotspot inside the van. Log into your van's wi-fi network with your phone, tablet or smart TV and Bob's your Wotzit.

In our experience, it does a superb job. Our unscientific tests suggest the same SIM card produces around twice the download and upload speeds when it's in the router compared to when it's in a phone being used inside the van.

However, don't expect miracles. These systems can only boost a weak mobile signal. They don't work if there's no signal to boost.

BOOSTING CAMPSITE WI-FI

Our router has another trick up its sleeve. If your campsite's wi-fi network is unbearably slow, your booster should in theory be able to pick up and amplify the campsite's wi-fi signal.

Some systems will do an excellent job, but we have struggled with ours. For starters, it doesn't automatically tune into the campsite wi-fi network. We must programme in all the fiddly network details into the router. We like to think we are pretty tech savvy, but we found the entire process a bit clunky.

We've called the product helpline on several occasions, and the company has always been extremely supportive, but we've never managed to access a campsite wi-fi when we needed to. The instructions that come with the device do suggest it's probably only worth trying to log on if you are staying in one place, on one campsite network, for a time.

They also point out that our version will never work if you must access campsite wi-fi through a portal – i.e., if you've got to go onto the campsite website to log into the wi-fi, and even make a payment.

Maybe this technology is still developing. Maybe have been unlucky and just picked sites with poor or inappropriate wi-fi networks. However, we've given up trying to make this feature work and rely solely on the device to boost mobile signals, which, as I've said, it does exceptionally well – even in some truly remote places. If you buy one, maybe get the supplier to demonstrate that it *will* boost a wi-fi signal.

MOBILE DATA IN EUROPE

We really struggled to get enough affordable, reliable mobile data during our first stint of European travel. Looking back, I think we just assumed it would be easy. It wasn't.

This whole area of mobile data and phone packages is incredibly competitive and ever-changing. That's why I can't give any detailed advice on deals. Also, mobile phone companies seem to change their policies more often than their pants, so any recommendations I give would certainly be out of date as soon as you read them.

The most help I can offer is some general pointers based on our experiences.

One thing I am certain about. We needed far more mobile data than we ever imagined we would – not just for downloading films and TV programmes, but for essentials like banking and the many maps and apps we came to rely on for our life on the road. Mobile data is not a luxury for van life. It's an essential.

MOBILE CALLS AND DATA CHECKLIST

Before you travel, contact your existing mobile supplier and check where you stand on data usage (including any data caps) and international call charges (including roaming charges) in the specific countries you intend to visit.

We're convinced we remember hearing lots of assurances that Brexit would not affect things like roaming charges when we Brits use our phones in Europe. In our experience, that does not seem to be the case. The most annoying thing to look out for are those caps. This is when, no matter how much data you've bought, there's a limit to how much of it you can use, per month, if you stray outside your home country.

EUROPEAN DATA SIM CARDS

If you're buying a new data SIM in the UK to take into Europe, again, check if there are any caps on that data in the countries you intend to visit.

If you find a data SIM deal online that requires a physical SIM card, for your phone or wi-fi router, it's likely the SIM will have to be delivered to your home address. So, this definitely needs sorting before you leave.

An alternative is to buy a pay-as-you go SIM in each country you visit.

When our first data package ran out much faster than we expected, we did some online research and got a cracking deal in Sweden. We walked into a tobacconist in Stockholm and bought a 100GB SIM with no strings attached.

Our Swedish SIM card deal was so good, we still had data left when we crossed into Norway. Then, of course, we were "roaming" from Sweden and our data was capped. Curses.

We have read that some countries or phone companies won't allow you to buy any kind of SIM unless you supply a social security number for that country – which of course you don't have if you don't live there. The rules appear to be tightening on this, so again, it may well be easier to source a a deal and SIM at home before your travel.

However, in other countries, however, the mobile networks are more helpful. In Albania and Montenegro we unexpectedly got great data deals on "tourist" SIM packages. Spending around £15 for £100GB in Montengro was the best deal on our trip.

I wish I could be more specific in this section, but this really is one of those areas where it's worth putting in the research in plenty of time before you go abroad.

Check the latest deals on the internet, or grit your teeth, pour a large whisky, and join the helpline call or online chat queue to talk to your mobile provider. It will be worth the effort if it means you avoid running out of data, being charged over the odds, and generally being stung for staying connected with the rest of the world when you're travelling.

BANKING AND PAYING FOR STUFF

Once again, I'm going to chicken out of giving detailed advice on banking arrangements for your big trip. There are so many variables depending on which bank you use, which countries you're visiting etc. However, I do have some general tips based on our discoveries.

First, it's likely your existing bank cards will work throughout Europe when you're withdrawing cash or paying for goods directly. The problem is that you may pay through the nose for the privilege.

Your bank may charge you a fee for each transaction abroad. Worse, and more likely, they may also add a currency conversion fee every time you use your card in another country. Our existing banks walloped us in this way.

Before we left, Steve shopped around and found Starling Bank, a purely online bank that charged no fees whatsoever for transactions abroad. We're not affiliated with Starling in any way but are happy to recommend them.

For convenience, we've kept our original bank accounts, but don't use them abroad. Instead, we transfer money into our new "travel" account – and make all our overseas payments using our Starling cards. They worked in every country we visited and we had no conversion or transaction charges on our entire trip.

Other banks will offer similar terms. But as with mobile SIM cards I mentioned earlier, it's important to get any new accounts set up before you leave the UK, as banks will only deliver cards to your home address.

6. STAYING SAFE & SECURE

In everyday life, I'm not the most cautious of people. I'm generally optimistic and this may result in me being a bit lackadaisical when it comes to safety and security. That sounds like I'm a liability. I'm not. I don't take needless risks; I just don't fret about awful things happening. Glad we've got that straight.

All that changed after a conversation with Steve's friend Sarah, a seasoned overseas campervanner and off-gridder. Shockingly, some low life tried to break into her van during the night while she and her partner were asleep in it! It happened at an official camper parking lot in Denmark. It's the first security issue she'd had in over thirteen years of travelling abroad, so we need to keep this in context. But it was enough to make me want to turn Cliff into a mobile Fort Knox.

The imaginings started. What if Cliff was stolen when we were four thousand miles from home on the top of an Italian mountain? What if some Albanian hooligan smashed Cliff's plastic windows, made off with our passports, and we'd never be allowed home again? I think psychologists call this catastrophising.

Sure, we had proper insurance. I'll explain some of the insurance issues that apply to long trips abroad later. But the biggest worry was the sheer impracticality and inconvenience of being without the vehicle we were so reliant upon, or some of the important items inside.

BE ALARMED

Cliff came into our lives with an immobiliser. Thirty seconds after the main ignition key has been removed, it automatically prevents the engine being re-started – unless you use the keys the vehicle was supplied with. Cliff had no factory fitted alarm.

We had the usual debate. Everyone ignores alarms when they go off, so what's the point of having one? Who would even hear an alarm if we'd parked the van in the depths of the Black Forest?

Of course, we did fit one, simply because we felt we had to take every sensible precaution. We went for a "motorhome" alarm fitted by a specialist supplier. Alarms and how they're fitted vary hugely, depending on their type, brand, and the specifics of your vehicle. Though from what we discovered, it seems slightly easier to add an alarm to a campervan than a motorhome.

Campers are created within the confines of standard vans. Therefore, the driver's door, passenger's door, rear doors and sliding side door are already wired to the system that warns you if you've left a door open. In very simple terms, an alarm can patch into this wiring "network" and all your doors are alarmed.

With most motorhomes, your driver and passenger doors are part of the original base vehicle's cab, so are likely to have the "you've left me open" sensors and wiring. But the side door to your accommodation block and the hatches to side lockers or a rear garage if you have one, are all part of a purpose-built structure that's been attached to the vehicle. These openings may have been wired for an alarm system but may not. If not, they're likely to need more wiring.

With many camper and motorhome alarms, you have the possibility of including a PIR movement sensor. These detect any movement in your van should, for example, an undesirable decide to ignore the alarmed doors and break in through a window or skylight.

There is an issue with PIRs at night. If you want to set the alarm while you're sleeping, the sensors will obviously detect any movement inside the van. So, a trip to the loo or any movement by your dog, for example, will trigger the alarm and wake the dead.

So, top tip again - make sure you buy an alarm with the type of PIR sensor that can be disabled, while still allowing the door alarms to be active. PIRs are usually disabled by a specific button on your alarm fob, or by a separate fob that slips into a slot on your dashboard. Our system, with a remote fob, cost what I felt was reasonable £550.

BEAR STRAPS

I know this is overkill when we have an alarm, but we also use "bear straps" when we're sleeping or parking the van in a location that's isolated or feels the remotest bit dodgy.

I should also mention that we have a golden rule that if either one of us has any negative feelings about a place we pull up at, hoping to stay the night, we don't stay. No argument, no discussion... just move on.

Back to our bear straps. We gave them this name after making the slightly surprising discovery that wild bears roam the forests in Sweden. Not very many of them, admittedly, but let's not take any chances.

Should any rampaging bear decide it wants to break into our campervan through the driver or passenger doors, it is sure to be thwarted by a band of strong, black webbing that we loop through the arm rests and secure with a buckle. It becomes impossible to open either door from the outside.

A set of straps cost less than a tenner online. Their proper names, if you're searching the internet include cargo, ratchet, tensioning or lashing straps.

DOOR LOCK REINFORCEMENT

This next security measure is a reaction to reading scare stories online. If you do any research around Fiat Ducato security, you'll soon come across claims that the standard door locks are not as villain-proof as they should be. It seems thieves in the know can force the locks easily. Obviously, I won't say exactly how it's done, but if I could discover how online, so can undesirables.

A solution is to fit high-grade, stainless-steel plates to all your door handles. These are specially made for the Fiat Ducato and its Citroen and Peugeot cousins. They consist of an outer plate that sandwiches between your plastic door handle and the metal door skin. A second metal plate goes on the back of the handle, inside the door cavity, to shield the locking mechanism. You'll find these devices advertised as "Pro Plates," or "anti-break-in lock/handle guards" accompanied by confident claims they can be fitted with no drilling or use of adhesives.

The set of four plates I ordered cost £120. Using the clear instructions supplied, I managed to fit plates to the rear doors and sliding side door easily. The cab doors are far tricker, because you have to remove all the plastic panels and door fittings without breaking any mouldings or losing any screws or clips.

While the passenger door took some time, the driver's door was in another league. Its lock includes the central locking mechanism. I ended up having to use a hack saw to increase the size of the hole in the internal plate that was supplied - not the easiest job when you're trying to cut through hardened steel.

Fitting it wasn't easy either. All that extra central locking paraphernalia around the lock made it a physical challenge because I could hardly get my fingers into the tiny spaces.

I got there in the end and the result doesn't spoil the look of the vehicle. The plates are only just visible but will act as a deterrent as well as ensuring your door handles are much harder to tamper with. If you're tempted to add this extra layer of security, make sure you order the right product for your van's type and model year. They do vary slightly.

VEHICLE TRACKER

Campervans and motorhome are extremely desirable and therefore very stealable items. Thefts are reported to have increased dramatically when demand for leisure vehicles reached new heights during the COVID pandemic. And although it happens rarely, motorhomes with alarms, steering locks or pedal locks have been hauled away by professional thieves equipped with a tow trucks. Bar stewards.

We bit the bullet and decided to have a vehicle tracker fitted. A very enthusiastic engineer turned up and buried a tracker transmitter in a top-secret location deep inside our van. He only agreed to tell me roughly where he'd squirrelled it away after I bought him a sandwich.

The idea is that the transmitter is so well hidden and inaccessible that anyone stealing the vehicle would never be able to find the device to remove or disable it. Satellites pick up the transmitter signal and can locate your vehicle 24/7. You pay a subscription for the service, and you can log into an app to find your van on a live map.

I passed the app details and our log-in details to my grown-up kids, who, uncharacteristically, were a little un-nerved by my plan to drive away for a year with no fixed plan. They were able to see exactly where I was whenever they wanted. Yes, my civil liberties were infringed, but it stopped them fretting.

Thankfully, we've not had cause to use the tracking system for anything untoward. Though I did get warning text messages on a couple of occasions that my vehicle had been moved. Both times, I worked out that it was when Cliff had been on the open deck of a ferry in Norway. The satellites must have tracked that he was moving while his engine was switched off. He wasn't being towed away by villains. Good to know the system works.

SAFE OR STRONG BOX?

My final paranoia centred on our passports, bank cards, phones or watches being stolen from the van. A cash tin or portable strong box seemed a pointless idea. Thieves could simply walk off with either of these and blow them up with explosives.

What we needed was a safe or strong box physically attached to the van. Cliff has a few, under-floor storage compartments. The biggest, although shallow, looked like the ideal place to secure a safe. Despite much research, I couldn't find any campervan safe or other form of strongbox that had the right dimensions.

Then I discovered a safe designed for the very space I had in mind by Sunlight's sister campervan brand, Corado. It would have cost more than I could justify, and besides, I couldn't get my hands on one. The COVID effect still meant so many parts and accessories for campers were on back order with no guaranteed dates for supply.

So, in the end, I found a small, surprisingly lightweight safe – a bit like those you find in hotel room wardrobes. It had a digital keypad lock system, and I was able to attach it securely in a location that shall remain secret. Enormous peace of mind came from *Argos* for a mere £40.

So, with all these gadgets and gismos, we were a secure as we felt we needed to be.

BREAKDOWN COVER

As Cliff was a new Fiat Camper, he came with three years of *Fiat Campervan Assist* cover. One quick call to an emergency hotline should get us help if we had the misfortune to breakdown anywhere in Europe.

If you have existing breakdown cover, it's well-worth checking that it covers the parts of Europe you intend to visit. If you don't have any, I'd suggest you get some.

We rang Campervan Assist after the scariest night we've ever had in a gale force wind on the top of a Norwegian Mountain. More on that story in later books about our travels. As we came down the mountain the next morning, an amber warning light lit up on the dash. It said there was a problem with our stop/start system, and we needed to check the engine.

Amber warnings tend not to induce panic attacks when you're driving around Britain. There's always some kind of garage or professional help nearby. Being in a remote region of a foreign country and relying on your van for your very existence makes it a whole different matter.

We limped to a petrol station and waited for the Norwegian version of an AA engineer to turn up. We expected someone who would whip out their diagnostic tool, have a bit of a tinker, re-set the system, and tell us it was safe to go on our way.

Instead, a giant flat-backed truck arrived. It had the name NAF sign-written on the side of it. The polite engineer explained that he didn't do *any* roadside repairs. He didn't even have a diagnostic tool.

All he could do was put Cliff on the back of his lorry and deposit him (and us) at the nearest Fiat dealership. As it was Saturday, we'd have been in a dealership car park for two nights.

Instead, we decided to risk driving on. The engineer re-assured us that an amber light wasn't critical, but if it went red, we should stop. We vowed to call at the next Fiat Commercial dealership on our route to have things checked out.

I'm recounting this simply to underline that the roadside assistance we're accustomed to in the UK is a bit of a rarity in mainland Europe. They tend *not* to repair at the roadside, just scoop up your vehicle and take it to a dealership to fix.

It's also worth mentioning that after a few hours of driving, the warning light went out – and fifteen thousand miles later (as I write this), it has not come back on again. "Bloomin' Fiats," I hear my dad mutter.

TOOL KIT & OIL

In addition to having breakdown recovery in place, we thought we'd better prepare for more simple, routine issues that might affect our van. I bought a compact toolkit from Halfords; the biggest pack of assorted electrical fuses you've ever seen (I've not needed one of them); a tyre pressure gauge and a large bottle of the extremely specific vintage of motor oil that Cliff drinks.

I'd read more internet scare stories suggesting any deviation from the precise spec of oil could invalidate Cliff's warranty if his engine blew up, for example. So, I spent a ridiculous amount of money buying a bottle of oil direct from my local Fiat Professional Dealership. I've since found it cheaper on Amazon. You'll need to check your vehicles owner's manual to be certain which type of oil your specific camper's engine runs on.

And yet another top tip - buy a cheap funnel to help you pour oil into your engine. There's no room in our engine bay to get the oil bottle anywhere near the inlet on the top of the engine, so without a funnel, the liquid gold spills everywhere.

SPARE WHEEL AND TYRE

A spare wheel was not top of my accessory list during the exciting days when we were choosing Cliff. But I was a bit dismayed to discover (afterwards) that not only did he not have one, he didn't have anywhere to put one. It seems they're far from standard on campervans and motorhomes, but we dare not tackle a year long trip into some very remote regions without a spare. Plus, in some countries, it's a legal requirement to carry one.

First, I sourced a spare wheel cradle, with a winch, which attaches to the chassis behind the rear axle. I managed to install it myself. It wasn't too difficult, as the bolts that were supplied fitted into pre-drilled holes in the chassis.

Then I sourced a spare wheel to sit inside the cradle. This was a little tricker than I expected. The wheel you need depends on which Fiat (or other) chassis your camper or motorhome has been built on. There are many variants. You need to make sure the holes in your spare wheel match the studs on your wheel hubs. The simplest solution is to contact a dealership and give them your chassis number. They'll tell what spec you need for your spare wheel.

SNOW CHAINS/ SNOW TYRES

While a few flakes of snow bring the UK to a standstill, areas of Europe accustomed to severe winter weather like to keep things moving. That's why many countries recommend, or demand you fit winter tyres and/or carry snow chains.

Countries that require you to carry snow chains and use them where signs dictate in their mountainous regions include France, Germany, Sweden, Switzerland, Norway, Italy, Austria, Andorra and Albania.

You only fit the chains when there's snow on the ground - otherwise you get into bother for damaging the road surface.

The precise rules and regulations on winter tyres and snow chains vary widely from country to country and between regions within countries. France, for example, has recently allowed 48 of its local government areas in mountainous areas to set their own local rules. From 2022, non-compliance in some areas could result in fines of around £116.

So, it's advisable to check the latest regulations in any regions you plan to visit between October and March. This RAC web page is a useful tool. https://www.rac.co.uk/drive/travel/driving-in-europe/winter/

We only realised we needed snow chains the day before we were due onboard *Le Shuttle* to France. We had the devil's own job sourcing some. You'll find plenty for cars, but campers and motorhomes are based on commercial vehicles, so need chains that are a bit bigger and rarer, it seems.

You can buy, mail order, from online specialists, but we'd run out of time for that. We were extremely lucky to find a supplier just five minutes off our route to the Channel Tunnel. So we grabbed a pair for £125 (you only need them for the two driving wheels) and the salesman checked they were the right size. Incidentally, they weighed a ton.

A cheaper and lighter alternative is snow socks. They're made from a strong fabric and fit over your tyres to give extra grip in ice and snow. The specialists I called said they weren't as effective as chains and were a "bit of a grey area" when it came to the laws around Europe. Going for chains was a last-minute expense we could have done without, but at least we were covered for all eventualities and didn't panic every time we saw roadside snow chain warning signs on our travels.

OTHER EQUIPMENT

You're likely to need a few more pieces of equipment on board your campervan or motorhome to comply with driving regulations in Europe. Here's a *basic* checklist:

* Reflective jackets, kept in the cabin - one for each occupant of the vehicle.

* Warning triangles to place on the road in case of breakdown or accident. These are compulsory in most countries.

* Headlamp beam deflectors. These need to be stuck on the

headlamps of UK, right-hand-drive vehicles to allow safe driving on the right side of the road in Europe. They prevent your lights dazzling oncoming drivers.

* UK stickers on your vehicle, if you don't have a UK Euro number plate. However, some countries including Spain, Cyprus and Malta require you to have a sticker, whatever it says on your plate.

For up-to-date requirements for the countries you're visiting, check: https://www.gov.uk/foreign-travel-advice

7. BLOOMIN' PAPERWORK

I know van life is about escaping from humdrum stuff like paperwork. But you're much more likely to chillax on your trip if you can clear up a few travel admin issues before you go.

This chapter is a bit of a checklist of things to sort out for you and your van.

INSURING YOUR CAMPER OR MOTORHOME

We traded in our car to buy our first Vee-dub campervan and thought it would be a case of transferring our existing motor insurance to our camper. Wrong. Insurance policies for leisure vehicles are completely different from those for cars. High street insurance companies don't always understand the camper and motorhome market, so it usually pays to insure through a specialist broker.

They've heard all the issues before, have the experience to ask the right questions and know which insurance companies can provide the cover you need. They can even tackle more complex cover when you may be insuring a self-built camper, for example.

INSURANCE OVERSEAS

Even if you've got insurance in place, don't assume that it will cover you for travel abroad – especially if you're planning an extended trip.

Policies vary. Ours allows us to spend 180 days abroad in any year's insurance cover. Specifically, it gives us the minimum legal cover needed in any EU country, plus countries signed up to the EU's Directive on Insurance of Civil Liabilities arising from the use of motor vehicles (number 2009/103/EC) – whatever that may be.

We knew that our trip may involve more than 180 days, and resolved to update our insurers and be prepared for additional cover when our plans and travel dates had firmed up.

What we hadn't bargained on was an enforced stay *outside* the EU - for irritating and frustrating travel restriction reasons explained in Chapter 10. In short, we ended up having to spend 90 days in Albania - which is not in the EU, and therefore not covered by our existing insurance.

A specialist we were referred to refused to give us a quote for Albania until a month before we were due to go there - because "situations keep changing." And when we did finally get a quote, it was a staggering £1,044. Yes... just over a thousand pounds for 90 days comprehensive cover in Albania (plus Montenegro and Slovenia to be accurate).

We tried to get alternative quotes, but even SAGA who are well known for insuring campers and motorhomes refused to touch Albania. Also, the broker I have used for years tried the three insurers they use for mobile homes, and none of them could help either. It made us wonder what the problem was with Albania, and knocked our confidence about going there to be honest.

We had a choice; either bite the bullet and pay up, or go home early and spend three months driving around Ireland and the UK.

Now, of course, you may not wish to go to Albania. I include this cautionary tale simply to flag up that straying out of the EU can cause insurance complications.

We discovered two golden rules. First, be upfront about your plans and give your insurers as much information as you can about where you're going and, if possible, when.

Try go get all your insurance issues sorted before you set off on your travels. It's likely to cost you more to adapt or add to you insurance once your trip is underway.

And, of course, make sure you take your insurance certificate and policy documents with you.

As with most of the paperwork in this chapter, it's an idea to have scans or photos of important documents on your phones as well as carrying hard copies.

MOTOR INSURANCE GREEN CARD

There's no need to worry about having a "green card" if you're sticking to EU countries, or Ireland, Andorra, Bosnia and Herzegovina, Iceland, Liechtenstein, Norway, Serbia, and Switzerland.

However, if you're venturing into Albania, Azerbaijan, Belarus, Moldova, Russia, Turkey, Ukraine, or a host of other countries – you may need one. (Our £1000+ insurance cover for Albania included a Green Card. Much appreciated!)

What are they? Well, they're not green for a start – and haven't been since the 1960s. They're not additional insurance you need to take out either. They are a really simple document that confirms which countries you are covered for. They're so simple,they get over any language barriers you might have at a border, if you're involved in an accident or stopped by the police.

Yes, I know, you'll have a certificate of insurance, but in some countries, that's simply not enough.

Most insurance companies will issue you with a green card, for free, on request. The card may be posted out to you, but our insurers sent ours out via email, and we were able to print out a hard copy at a print shop.

The easiest way to check which countries require green cards is to visit the UK government website: https://www.gov.uk/vehicle-insurance/driving-abroad

You may need additional green cards if you're towing a trailer or have more than one insurance policy covering your trip.

INTERNATIONAL DRIVING PERMIT

And in case your van's onboard filing cabinet wasn't full enough, you may need an International Driving Permit or IDP.

If your travels will be confined to the EU, you can forget about IDPs. EU countries don't require them. Nor does Switzerland, Norway, Iceland, or Liechtenstein. However, they're either required or recommended in around 140 other countries. To get the latest information on where they are required, check the UK government web page:

https://www.gov.uk/driving-abroad/international-driving-permit

If you *do* need an IDP, there's another complication. There are three distinct types: a 1926, a 1959 and a 1968. Different countries require different IDPs. So, you may need more than one, depending on which countries you are intending to drive through.

You apply for them, in person, at UK Post Offices that offer "international driving permit" in their list of services. You'll need your UK (card) driving licence and a passport standard photo to apply. If you have the old-style paper driving licence, you'll need to show your passport too. Each IDP costs £5.50.

We weren't asked to show our IDPs at any point on our journey. But that's not to say you won't be.

SERVICING, INSPECTIONS AND WARRANTIES

Our planned departure date coincided with Cliff's first birthday. The anniversary meant he needed a service at a main Fiat Professional Dealership to ensure the vehicle warranty and "Campervan Assist" rescue cover remained valid.

We booked the service months in advance, knowing that our local Fiat Professional dealership had been struggling with demand during COVID, a time when, understandably, servicing the local fleet of Fiat Ducato-based NHS ambulances took priority.

Since then, we've discovered even motorhome dealers can struggle to get vehicles booked in for service and repairs.

Now COVID is less of an excuse, it seem it's because garages that look after commercial vehicles prioritise customers with service contracts – the likes of hauliers and couriers who have fleets of vehicles needing regular attention.

I have found it much more difficult to get Cliff booked in for servicing, repair work or quick inspections than any car I've owned. It may still be the aftermath of COVID, but I'd strongly suggest you make bookings for camper or motorhome servicing well in advance of when you need them.

It's a similar story when it comes to annual water ingress inspections. Cliff also needed one of these, from a Sunlight dealer, around his first anniversary, if the Sunlight warranties on the camper conversion were to remain valid.

The inspection is a quick (£100) check to make sure the campervan body is not leaking. Drilling holes for skylights, vents, and cable holes in the roof of a van isn't the ideal way to keep them watertight.

Workshops at motorhome dealerships can also become stacked out with work at certain times of the year - mostly in Spring when everyone wants to get their mobile homes back on the road for the new season. So again, book earlier than you'd ever think you'd need to.

We scheduled our water ingress inspection for the day before we set off on our big trip. A bit late in the day, I know. However, our supplying dealer was two hundred miles from home, for reasons I've explained earlier. Our nearest Sunlight dealer declined to do work on our van, as at that time, they were prioritising vehicles they had supplied.

We'd assumed a "network" of dealerships for campervans would work like a network of car dealerships. Buy a Ford car and you can take it into any official Ford dealer to have warranty work done. Not necessarily the case in the camper and motorhome market it seems.

So, the moral of our story, again, is buy your campervan from a dealership that's close to you if humanly possible. I should add that our supplying dealers, Goodman's in Waltham Abbey, Essex, have responded brilliantly to warranty issues. It's not their fault that, for us, visiting them involves us in a 400-mile round trip.

Anyhow, with the service and inspection done, Cliff's warranties were intact and he was as ready as he could be for the epic journey ahead.

OTHER VEHICLE DOCUMENTS

Make sure you take your camper or motorhome's logbook (DVLA V5 document) on your travels. It proves you own the vehicle and confirms its emissions standard, should anyone need to know. Border guards asked for our V5 in Montengro and North Macedonia.

This may seem a bit over the top, but it may be worth having a copy of your original purchase invoice, just so there's no doubt your mobile home belongs to you.

And don't forget to take your vehicle owner's manual and all the instruction booklets for the various accessories and gadgets on board. You'd be surprised how many times we've had to refer to them when things went wrong or didn't work. Or maybe you wouldn't.

PASSPORTS

Who would set off on a foreign trip without their passport? Well, me actually. Years ago, my forgetfulness almost kiboshed a family trip to Florida. But that's another story.

If you're planning a big trip in a camper or motorhome, your passport must be valid in every country you visit. What counts as valid varies from country to country, though it usually relates to when your passport expires. Most EU countries need at least three months on your passport *after* you've left their borders.

The only way to be sure is to check up-to-date passport requirements for the countries you intend to visit on the UK government's web page: https://www.gov.uk/guidance/foreign-travel-checklist

I had to renew my passport before our big trip. The whole process was very efficient and took around two weeks. I even received reassuring update texts throughout the process. But there have been periods when the passport office has struggled to process applications. So, play safe and give yourself plenty of time.

If you're travelling after October 2023, you'll also need to have registered on The European Travel Information and Authorisation System - ETIAS. I'll explain more about this new online security check in chapter ten. Successful applications are automatically linked to your passport.

TRAVEL & HEALTH INSURANCE

You'll need travel and health insurance for a big trip, just as you do for a standard holiday abroad. Just make sure it covers all the destinations on your itinerary and the full period you intend to travel.

There may be some overlap between your motorhome policy and travel insurance when it comes to covering personal items against theft etc. To avoid any confusion and any important items not being covered, do check through the small print. Boring - but essential.

When it comes to taking out health insurance, it's complex and highly personalised. Definitely one for an experienced insurance company or broker.

However, even if you have a health insurance policy, make sure you're also entitled to mostly free "necessary healthcare" in all the EU countries you visit.

Although we Brits have left the EU, the Brexit Withdrawal Agreement still entitles us to "necessary healthcare" at GPs and state-run hospitals in EU countries (plus Switzerland) – providing we're on a temporary visit and can produce an EIHC (European Health Insurance Card) or GIHC (Global Health Insurance Card).

These are particularly useful if you have any kind of accident or emergency.

EIHC cards are being phased out for us Brits, but if you have one that's still valid, you can use it. If not, you need to apply for a new GHIC card.

Just search online for "NHS applying for healthcare cover abroad" and complete the GHIC application form. (See links in Appendix 1). The card is free from the NHS. Be careful not to visit carbon copy websites that may charge a fee simply to forward a card from the health service. Once issued, a GHIC is valid for five years.

State healthcare isn't always free in EU countries. The rule is that you'll be expected to pay whatever citizens of each country would pay. And while GHIC cards *can* be used in non-EU Switzerland under a special arrangement, since Brexit, they are no longer valid in Iceland,

Liechtenstein, and Norway. All the rules and conditions can be access through the official NHS website.

One word of warning - do all you can to put any additional health insurance in place before you set off on your travels. A few companies do allow you to take out policies when you're "already travelling" - but it'll cost you considerably more than if you'd put the cover in place before you left home.

COVID VACCINATION RECORDS

COVID and the rules and restrictions around it are forever changing. How's that for an understatement. We visited twenty countries (July 2022 to July 2023) and were never asked for any vaccination records. The only time we were required to wear masks was while travelling on some city metro systems.

But any country could introduce travel restrictions at very short notice in response to the ever-changing challenges of the virus. So, always check the local situation in the country you intend to visit. You'll find detailed, up-to-date information at: https://www.gov.uk/foreign-travel-advice

The most useful actions you can take before you travel are to make sure your COVID vaccinations are up to date and have evidence of your vaccination history in the form of an NHS COVID pass.

The pass is available online or by using the NHS App. You can have it sent to you via email, display it on your smartphone, have it sent in an email or print it out. This official NHS record should be accepted as evidence of your COVID vaccination status in any country you visit.

8. PLANNING & PREPARING TO TRAVEL

As I've mentioned, the double-whammy of Brexit then COVID delayed the start of our big trip by at least two years. Did we use this lengthy delay to plan our adventure in the minutest detail? Of course not.

On the morning we finally packed the last few essentials into Cliff and handed the keys for the flat to the rental agent, our diary for the first leg of our expedition was to all intents and purposes blank.

The only entries were the check-in times and reservation numbers for our outward ferry crossing from Harwich to the Hook of Holland on July 1st, and the details of our return voyage on September 23rd.

We had booked a campsite for the first two nights of our adventure, close to the Dutch port. Our easy start was designed to help us recover from chaos of the previous week packing our lives into storage boxes; acclimatise to driving our right-hand-drive campervan on the wrong side of the road and get our heads around what had just happened.

Apart from that, the diary pages were blank. I do appreciate that this degree of freedom is the stuff of lifelong dreams. But for me, who may be a bit of a control freak, the stark reality of absolutely zilch stretching out in front of me for at least twelve weeks caused a tightening of the stomach and some involuntary clenching.

We'd made a deliberate decision not to pin down any details of the trip, and for once in our lives, go with the flow. But we had thought enough about the trip to have an exceptionally lengthy list of locations and attractions we were excited to visit.

At that early stage, our probable route had no more than a viewed-from-space level of detail. It consisted of a vague line leaving the Hook of Holland, heading East through the Netherlands and Northern

Germany to the port of Rostock. There, we thought we'd catch a ferry across the Baltic Sea to Trelleborg on Sweden's south coast.

Once in Scandinavia, we'd drive all the way up the East Coast before crossing into Norway, then North as far as anyone can go on the European mainland to Nordkapp. Taking a campervan to the same latitude as Siberia felt epic.

Our return journey would bring us down the West Coast of Norway, taking in the glorious Lofoten Islands. After nipping back into Sweden we'd cross the giant bridge we'd seen on those gruesome TV dramas into Denmark, and after exploring Dane Land, head back to the ferry port via Germany and Holland.

It was a framework. The details would be filled in on a day-to-day basis. This is where I must pay full tribute to my better half. Steve had spent weeks on the internet, scouring informal travel blogs, official tourism websites and YouTube channels, building up a comprehensive list of potential destinations in the countries we planned to visit.

Over time, certain locations rose to the surface of the ideas pool and became must-see favourites. These places became pins stuck in our imaginary route map; key points we knew we wanted to visit but had no idea how or when.

In practise, after we visited one of these milestones, we'd plumb the next one into the sat nav and map out the next section of our route. Then, we'd go back to Steve's wish list to see how many other amazing towns or cities, spectacular viewpoints, interesting museums, galleries, fun parks, and stunning beaches we could cram in over the next leg of our journey.

Our haphazard approach to planning often involved diversions and even circular loops when we messed things up. But we hardly missed any destination that had caught our interest, plus we discovered lots of unexpected gems off the tourist trail.

And besides, what could possibly go wrong? We had electronic devices and apps to help us. I'm listing them here so they could help you right from the start of your trip.

SAT NAV

It may be the most obvious gadget to take on a marathon road trip through unknown countries, but I can't emphasise enough that our adventure would have been impossible without sat nav.

It doesn't matter what brand you have, just make sure it includes European maps and is fully updated before you set off. Downloading sat nav maps swallows up vast amounts of data, so best do this using your home wi-fi connection if you can.

Our device is a TomTom Camper Go – a version that allows you to plumb in the dimensions of your campervan, so, it can avoid sending you along roads or under bridges that are too small for your vehicle. In theory.

We've christened our dashboard guide "Shaughness," because we set him to direct us across Europe in dulcet Irish tones.

During the first 10000-miles of our trip, our electronic Irishman hardly put a foot wrong. I've used sat nav for decades, but still marvel at what detail is included in their unfathomably enormous maps – from the remotest track in the Arctic Circle to the smallest backstreets in major cities.

We wouldn't have dared drive into the likes of Hamburg, Oslo, Copenhagen, Le Mans or the outskirts of Rome without clear directions from Shaughness.

His constant display of the speed limits proved as useful his directions. You can read up on the generic speed limits for each country you visit, but it's easy to forget the general rules or miss specific road signs when you're under pressure – i.e., driving, on the wrong side of the road, in unfamiliar surroundings.

We found speed limits displayed on the device matched those on road signs accurately for most of our journey.

Shaughness was less reliable in Norway where he either took a while to register changes in speed limits, or simply got them wrong on a number of roads. No idea what was going on there. We did update him before we set off.

We also thought he'd had a seizure on a German Autobahns when the speed limit disappeared completely from his screen. It wasn't his fault – we were on one of those famed sections of motorway where there are no speed restrictions at all. Duh!

But we did feel a bit let down by our dashboard-mounted friend while travelling through Albania, Montengro and Slovenia. After too many failures to find locations and taking us down roads that were unsuitable for Sherman tanks let alone campervans, our bond of trust was broken. We found using Google maps on our phone more reliable in these countries.

WHERE TO CAMP

Without doubt, the single most useful app we used throughout our trip was Park4Night. The basic version is free to download onto your mobile phone and displays thousands of locations that are of specific interest to anyone with a camper, motorhome, or caravan.

These include official campsites, places to fill up with drinking water, grey waste disposal sites, facilities for emptying toilet waste and even the location of LPG stations. You can search for facilities "near me" – or by selecting specific areas on a map.

For us, the most invaluable feature was being able to search for locations where we could overnight for free. Scandinavia has a different attitude to the UK when it comes to accessing the countryside. There's a lot of misunderstanding about the rules in Europe and the UK, so there's much more detail in chapters ten and eleven.

It's not an exaggeration to say that in allowing us to make the most of free parking spots, the Park4Nigth App made huge sections of our trip possible and affordable.

Each of its location listings includes reviews and ratings from people who've stayed there before. The reviews translate from any language at the touch of a button. They're also dated, so you know how recently reviewers stayed at the site.

In the app, location details are given in postcodes, which can be a bit vague, as well as longitude and latitude co-ordinates which are more accurate. It turns out you can input detailed co-ordinates into our sat nav's search bar. Who knew?

The free version of the Park4Night app is useful, but you'll find many more locations listed if you upgrade to the subscription version. It costs only £1.59 per month. It's ad free, runs on more types of devices and enables you to contact official campsites directly through the app. A bargain.

GOOGLE LENS

You may have come across Google Translate, where you type words into its app or website in one language and they're instantly translated into another.

Google Lens makes the process even easier using digital sorcery. Open this app on your smartphone and point your camera at any words you want to translate. It could be German gibberish on a parking sign or impenetrable Norwegian on a suspicious-looking packet of dried fish.

Whatever the language, the app will take a second to process, then superimpose an English translation on your screen, over the words you're trying to decipher. Genius.

LPG FINDER APP

I've mentioned earlier that mainland Europe doesn't really do the portable *Calor*-type gas tanks we're accustomed to in the UK. Instead, Euro campers and motorhomes tend to have permanent gas cannisters that you re-fill using the LPG equivalent of petrol pumps.

The challenge is that, even in Europe, LPG re-filling stations can be difficult to find. They're even rarer and more difficult to locate in remote, unpopulated areas – the kind of places folks love to go camping.

The Park4Night app includes locations of many LPG re-fill stations, but dedicated LPG apps tend to have more information. In Europe, we used MyLPG.eu.

Back home, we've found LPG pumps are not only rare, but have an annoying habit of being empty or broken, usually after you've travelled miles out of your way to find them. The AutogasApp UK includes the locations of pumps, confirms if they are working and the price of their LPG. There are also useful comments and tips from fellow LPG hunters who've used them.

ROAD, FERRY, AND BRIDGE TOLLS

This is not the place for a detailed look at tolls in Europe. That delight is saved for chapter twelve. However, it's worth noting that many countries that charge tolls have automated toll collection systems that you may wish to sign up to.

Simply, you register with your vehicle and bank details. Then, when you're travelling, roadside cameras recognise your number plate and charge you (usually monthly in arrears) for all the tolls you've incurred. The various schemes are mentioned in the country-by-country breakdown later. There's currently no single online account that will cover the whole of Europe.

9. WEIGHTY MATTERS

There I was, minding my own business, sat in my camping chair beside the van, gazing at the Elbe River upstream from Hamburg, munching a bacon butty. The Sunday morning peace was shattered by our German neighbour who'd arrived at the campsite the night before in a smart new motorhome.

"I think you have a bit of a weight problem," he declared, in slightly abrupt but otherwise perfect English.

His comment was not bacon butty related. He'd been staring at the back of our camper and concluded that the bodywork was sitting a bit low on the axle, suggesting we were overweight.

He was trying to be helpful and pointed out that being overweight wouldn't matter too much in Germany (that was entirely his opinion, and must not be taken as official advice), but warned that if we ventured into Italy, he was sure the police would wallop us with an enormous fine.

Before this encounter, I'd not really worried about Cliff being overweight. That said, he'd never been stuffed with enough gear for a year on the road before.

So, the seed of doubt and visions of rotting in an Italian jail cell were planted. I was concerned enough make a mental note to self; "Check out the maximum weight malarkey before Italy."

The weight of campervans, motorhomes and caravans is a serious matter, and something we should have got our heads around before we set off on our big trip.

Loading a van over its maximum permitted weight could make it unsafe to drive. Excess kilos can affect road handling, put a strain on key components like tyres and brakes and possibly invalidate your insurance if you have a disaster. Plus, our German friend was right - if you drive an overweight van, you could be fined.

But what weight should your van be? And how on earth do you find out what weight it is?

We encountered lots of confusing anacronyms and numbers when we tried to get to understand our weight issues. Hopefully, this chapter will make things a little clearer.

VEHICLE CLASSIFICATIONS – WHY IT MATTERS

Individual campervans and motorhomes are put into a certain class or category of vehicle, with weight playing a key part in which category they're put into. Your driving licence lists which categories of vehicle you're entitled to drive.

People with a standard car licence will be entitled to drive most campervans and motorhomes that fall into category B on a licence – that's vehicles up to a maximum weight of 3,500kg. Most mobile homes are built to be under this threshold, so they can be driven by most drivers.

Larger campers and motorhomes over 3,500 kg limit are in a different class. To drive vehicles that weigh between 3,500kg and 7,000kg, you will need to be entitled to drive category C1 on your licence.

If, like me, you passed your driving test before January 1st,1997 you should automatically have C1 entitlement on your licence. But if you got your full licence after this date, you'll have to pass an additional driving test to be entitled to drive one of these slightly bigger heavier motor homes.

If you want to get behind the wheel of the biggest of motorhomes, those "Meet-The-Fockers," American-style behemoths that are often built on a truck chassis, you will need to take a specific driving test to have category C put onto your licence. This is for vehicles that weigh over seven tonnes and is effectively an HGV or lorry driver's licence.

That is a simple overview. The rules are even more complex if you want to tow a trailer or a car, and there may be age-related restrictions on what you can drive, especially when you reach seventy. The best way to confirm your personal driving entitlement is to go to https://www.gov.uk/view-driving-licence, and check the details on your actual driving licence.

YOUR VEHICLE'S WEIGHT

So, we've established that your campervan or motorhome's vehicle classification tells you the most it's allowed to weigh if it's to be driven safely on the road. But that's a bit academic if you haven't a clue how much your vehicle actually weighs when it's fully loaded, fuelled, and with your family and the dog on board.

You could have a loaded van weighed at a weighbridge - and I'll come onto that in a moment. Or you could make some simple calculations that will be more convenient and at least warn you if you're heading towards the overweight danger zone.

MAXIUM SAFE WEIGHT

The starting point for your calculations is that maximum weight your camper or motorhome is allowed to be when it's fully loaded and remain safe to drive. It's known as its Maximum Allowable Mass (MAM) - the total weight of the vehicle, including the driver, passengers, fluids (fuel and water), cargo and any accessories that have been added to it.

Confusingly, there are a ridiculous number of names for this maximum weight which all mean pretty much the same thing. You may also see it referred to as:

* Gross Plated Weight

* Maximum Permissible Mass

* Maximum Permissible Laden Weight (MPLW)

* Gross Vehicle Weight (GVW)

* Maximum Technically Permissible Laden Weight (MPLW)

* Revenue Weight

The words mass and weight are interchangeable – so all these terms refer to the same thing.

The specific figure for your vehicle should be in the owner's manual and stamped on a metal Weight Plate inside the engine bay. It may also be on a sticker elsewhere in the vehicle. As an example, the MAM for our camper is 3,500 kg. This is what we expected given its vehicle classification.

Before we move on, I just want to add a special note about the Maximum Allowable Mass of the hugely popular VW campervan. They're a bit special, and confusing.

You could see three VW Transporter campers parked side by side, all the same wheelbase and to all intents and purposes identical. However, each of them could have a different Maximum Allowable Mass. That's because Transporter options include some vans built with beefed up brakes and suspension which allow them to carry more weight. They may or may not have badges on their back doors to help you out.

A van badged a T28 will have a Maximum Allowable Mass of 2,800kg. A T30 – 3,000kg and the T32, the maximum 3,200kg. If there are no external badges, the plate in the engine bay will reveal all.

WEIGHT WHEN EMPTY

A camper or motorhome's weight when it's empty is often called the Mass Running Order (MRO) or Mass In Running Order (MIRO). It's what the manufacturer or converter said your van weighed when it left the factory.

The figure should be listed in the blurb that comes with a new vehicle. If you're buying a used camper or motorhome, just ask the original manufacture for the MRO for your model if you can't find it. You may also see a reference to "Kerb Weight." This is what the van weighs when it's empty – without its driver but including fuel and standard equipment. Some manufacturers also quote a figure that includes an allowance for the driver.

One word of caution. The MRO may be the empty weight of a standard model that left the factory. If you've ordered (or someone has added) extra accessories like bike racks, an air con unit, extra leisure batteries, gas cannisters or water tanks - they may not be accounted for in the original "empty" weight, so you'll need to allow for them.

The MRO for our van is 2,700kg. So, in theory, the most weight we can add to our vehicle is the difference between its maximum allowed weight (3,500kg) and its weight when empty (2,700kg.) That's a maximum of 800kg spare capacity.

This capacity is often referred to as the payload. Very simply, it's the maximum weight of everything you can carry in your van. That's you, your family, food, beer, clothes, camping chairs, barbeques, bikes – everything.

TRAILERS AND WEIGHTS

Yes, there's more. You may also come across references to Gross Train Weight (GTW) or Gross Combination Weight (GCW). This refers to the total weight of a fully loaded campervan or motorhome, *plus* a fully loaded trailer. And remember, if you are pulling trailers, your driving licence categories will also determine what you're entitled to tow.

WEIGHBRIDGE SOLUTION

If this is all too complicated, you can take the maths and guesswork out of the equation by driving your camper or motorhome to a public weighbridge. If you're new to campervanning like us, it's unlikely you've needed a weighbridge at any point in your life – or even know what they are.

Think of them as a giant set of drive-on scales. They are mostly used by truck and van drivers who need to check or prove that their vehicles are not overloaded.

We had the good fortune, and astonishment, to come across a weighbridge at a roadside service station in Norway. We drove onto two metal plates that were sunk into the ground – front wheels on one plate, rear wheels on the other. As if by magic, and for free, the total weight of good old Cliff lit up on a digital display in front of us, as well as how that weight was split between the front and back axle.

It turns out our total weight was closer to the limit than we expected, but our diesel and freshwater tanks were full, so we reckoned we were as heavy as we were ever going to be. To be honest, having a figure was a tremendous relief and brought an end to those nightmares about ending up in an Italian jail.

Of course, you don't need to drive to Norway to have your campervan weighed. There are over five hundred public weighbridges across the UK. Most are run by local councils; some by private operators. It's likely you'll have to pay a small fee to use them.

The easiest way to find your nearest weighbridge in the UK is to use the DVLA's website. Just go to this webpage https://www.gov.uk/find-weighbridge - and type in your postcode.

There's no need to visit a weighbridge on a regular basis, but if you load your van up as you normally use it, you should at least get a benchmark of how much stuff you can carry on board while still being in safe driving limits.

SHEDDING THE KILOS

If after all this palaver you discover your camper or motorhome is close to or over the maximum allowed weight, it's time to shed the kilos. You could try the following diet:

* Diesel weighs just under 1kg (0.80kg) per litre, so consider filling your fuel tank half-way. It will mean more stops at forecourts, but it will reduce weight.

* Empty your fresh water before travelling and fill up when you reach your campsite. Our water tank holds 100 litres, weighing 100kg when it's full.

* Dump your wastewater before you drive too. Our tank holds 90kg of "grey" water.

* Consider buying smaller amounts of provisions en route rather than cramming your lockers and cupboards full of food and drink at the start of your journey.

10. ROAD TRIPPING IN THE SCHENGEN ZONE

Vanlife is supposed to be about freedom. That's probably why a set of pesky travel restrictions were the biggest and most irritating challenge on our year-long adventure.

These restrictions have only become an issue for Brits since Brexit. Ignoring them isn't an option. That could land you in the deepest of doo-doo.

So here's my attempt to explain the rather complicated travel restrictions for Brits in what's known as The Schengen Zone.

BREXIT IMPACT

Before Brexit, we Brits had the same rights to "freedom of movement" as all our EU cousins. We could travel anywhere in Europe for as long as we fancied - pretty much.

But when the UK left the EU, we lost this freedom and now face restrictions on how long we can spend in certain countries.

I should make it clear that you're unlikely to come up against any restrictions if you're a "short-term" visitor to most countries in Europe. That's someone who makes occasional, short trips for what you might consider a "normal" holiday.

The restrictions only kick in if you're going to be in any countries in the Schengen Zone for more than **90 days in any continuous 180-day period.**

That doesn't just impact people on long trips. It can also affect folks who pop in and out of Europe on a regular basis.

WHY ARE THERE TRAVEL RESTRICTIONS?

It all started back in 1985 when five European countries signed a pact called The Schengen Agreement. The mutual agreement was designed to make travel easier, abolishing border checks and controls between the countries involved.

Since then, more countries have signed up. As I'm writing this (August 2023), **27** countries are involved.

The UK has never been part of Schengen. Before Brexit, that wasn't a problem for Brits because we could enjoy the "freedom of movement" that came with our EU membership. We now face limits because we are in not in Schengen or the EU.

WHICH COUNTRIES HAVE RESTRICTIONS?

When we first heard about these potential restrictions, we assumed they applied to all the countries that remain in the European Union. But it turned out to be more complicated than that. Much more.

Most EU member countries *are* now in the Schengen Zone – but not all of them. Some are still waiting to join. And just to confuse us all further, some countries that are *not* members of the EU *have* signed up to the Schengen Agreement.

EU COUNTRIES IN THE SCHENGEN ZONE

There are currently, **23** EU countries in the Schengen Zone. They are:

Austria; Belgium; Croatia, The Czech Republic; Denmark; Estonia; Finland; France; Germany; Greece; Hungary; Italy; Latvia; Lithuania, Luxembourg; Malta; The Netherlands; Poland; Portugal; Slovakia; Slovenia; Spain and Sweden.

NON-EU COUNTRIES IN THE SCHENGEN ZONE

In addition, there are **four** countries which are not in the EU, but *have* signed up to the Schengen Agreement. They are:

Switzerland, Liechtenstein, Norway, and Iceland.

Gibraltar is a bit of an anomaly. As a British Territory, it left the EU when the UK did, and is not technically part of the Schengen Zone. But due to various special agreements – and the tiny island's position so close to the Spanish mainland, Gibraltar is treated as though it is part of the zone.

THE RESTRICTIONS - HOW THEY AFFECT YOU

If you're a citizen of a country that is not signed up to Schengen – like the United Kingdom – you are restricted to the amount of time you can spend in any countries in the Schengen Zone.

The basic "only 90 in 180 days" rule I mentioned earlier sounds quite simple. Brits are not allowed to stay anywhere within the Schengen Area for more than 90 days in any consecutive 180-day period.

In reality, working out what you're allowed to do can be a bit tricky. Luckily, there are many Schengen Calculators available online – on websites or on Apps - to help you out.

Using a calculator is simple. You just type in the dates and locations of recent trips you've made plus the dates and locations of any trip you are planning. Online magic will do the calculations and advise whether your up-coming trip is allowed. I've included a link to a Schengen calculators in Appendix 1.

COUNTRIES OUTSIDE THE SCHENGEN ZONE

Non-Schengen countries are ideal boltholes on long travels, because once you're in them, your Schengen calculator stops, and your days spent there don't eat into that 90 in 180 days allowance.

The United Kingdom is not the only country that is NOT part of the Schengen Zone.

Surprisingly, Ireland is not in Schengen, even though it *is* in the European Union. Ireland has opted out, apparently because its border with Northern Ireland would have made things too complicated.

Other EU countries that are currently outside the Schengen Zone are:

* Bulgaria - although it's legally obliged to join at some point.

* Cyprus - also legally obliged to join in future

* Ireland - likely to continue opting out

* Romania - also legally obliged to join in future.

The following countries are also **NOT** in the Schengen Zone.

Albania; Armenia; Azerbaijan; Belarus; Bosnia & Herzegovina; Kosovo; North Macedonia; Moldova; Montenegro; Serbia; Turkey and Ukraine.

Remember, you'll still have to make sure you meet each country's individual entry requirements for tourists.

THE ODDITIES

You won't be in the least bit surprised that there are a few anomalies.

If you think you can escape into microstates of Monaco, San Marino, and Vatican City to get out of Schengen...you can't. Technically, they're not in Schengen, but they don't impose border controls, so for all intents and purposes are considered part of the Schengen Zone. Remember also, GIbraltar is not a Schengen member but is treated as though it is.

LONGER STAY VISAS

There is one way for us Brits to stay in a specific Schengen country for more than 90 days - if we successfully apply for a longer stay or temporary residence visa, for that country.

The application process can be complicated and the criteria for granting these visas vary enormously from country to country. The details are too varied to list here, but often include proving you have sufficient funds to cover your stay. You may also be required to have a "sponsor" in the country you're applying to and give the address where you're staying. That can be tricky when the whole point of being on a campervan or motorhome adventure is that you don't have an address.

If you do decide to take the longer-term visa route, the key is to check the most up-to-date criteria for the specific country you've chosen and apply early. Each country's government website will usually have a section for travel and visas. Applications could take some time to process.

HOW IT WORKED FOR US

All this might make more sense if I explain how we managed to stay on the road in Europe for a year, and keep within the Schengen rules.

Phase 1 - Scandinavia (In Schengen)

We set off on July 1st, taking a ferry from Harwich to the Hook of Holland. We'd not travelled into any Schengen country for years, so had a full 90-day Schengen allowance to play with.

We had a cracking time travelling over seven thousand miles through Germany, Sweden, Norway, Denmark – then quickly back through Germany and the Netherlands to catch our ferry home.

This first leg of our trip was all in Schengen countries. By the time we got back to the Dutch docks, we'd totted up 85 days in the Schengen Zone. (We had deliberately stayed five days under the maximum 90-day allowance, just in case we hit any unexpected problems or delays.)

So, we came home to the spend Autumn and Christmas in the good old non-Schengen, UK.

Phase 2 - UK. (Not in Schengen)

Frankly, we'd have much preferred to head to the south of Spain for the winter as we could have done in pre-Brexit days. But having just spent 90 days in the Schengen Zone, it wasn't an option.

If we'd stayed in Schengen and gone over the 90-day limit, we could have been fined, imprisoned, or deported back to the UK. We may even have been banned from visiting any Schengen country again for several years. It's tricky to be precise about what could happen to you because individual Schengen countries come up with their own punishments for overstaying your welcome.

Having to explore the UK in our camper at the back end of the year wasn't ideal – but we had no choice. But by the time we reached Christmas, we had another ninety non-Schengen days under our belts. Our Schengen travel counter effectively zeroed, allowing us to head back into Europe .

Phase 3 - France, Spain and Italy (In Schengen)

The third leg of our trip took us through France, Spain, and Italy, which are all Schengen members. At the end of *that* 90-day stint we had to get out of Schengen again. See the pattern?

Phase 4 - Albania, North Macedonia & Montenegro (Not in Schengen)

For the fourth leg of our trip. we spent exactly 90 days in Albania, North Macedonia and Montenegro. These countries a currently not in the Schengen area, but are very keen to join. So they're unlikely to be an escape hole forever.

We spent most of our time in Albania which - to be honest - had not been on our bucket list. You can read the truth about exploring Albania in a camper or motorhome in my detailed blog at: vanlifevirgins.com.

Once we'd served our 90 days, we were free to enter the Schengen Zone again.

Phase 5 - Croatia, Slovenia, Austria, Switzerland, France (In Schengen)

Technically, we would have been allowed to travel through Schengen countries for yet another 90 days, but this last phase of our trip only lasted a few weeks. Our rental income from the flat was coming to an end and we needed to get home.

COMMON MISTAKES

There's no getting away from the fact that for long trips, this whole

Schengen business is complicated. Here are some of the most common mistakes people make.

* The Schengen Area restriction is 90 days in 180 days - *not* three months in six months. Months vary in length.

* Just because there is freedom to travel for 90 days, you still need a valid passport. What counts as "valid" varies in different countries, so you need to check that too.

* It's also crucial to get your passport stamped by border officials every time you enter or leave the Schengen Zone. Official stamps are the only evidence you'll have if you need to convince anyone where you have been and for how long.

And remember, the Schengen Area is constantly evolving, with new countries being admitted from time to time. Always check the latest information for any specific trip you're planning. The most reliable info is from the EU at: https://home-affairs.ec.europa.eu/policies/schengen-borders-and-visa/schengen-area_en

ETIAS

If your mind hasn't exploded already, there is one more change coming up that will affect European travel. It's called ETIAS - or The European Travel Information and Authorisation System. UK travellers are currently being recommended to apply for ETIAS before it becomes fully operational in November 2023. But what is it?

ETIAS is a not travel visa, but a system to digitally track travellers (like us) who currently travel visa-free into Europe, including Schengen area countries. Its main aim is to improve border security and identify anyone who may be a security risk.

Citizens of over sixty countries will need to apply for ETIAS, including the UK, America, Canada, and New Zealand.

Full details of the scheme are at https://www.schengenvisainfo.com/etias/

The website for applications is: https://www.etias.info/application/

ETIAS APPLICATION (KEY POINTS)

* You can only apply online.

* You will be asked to complete a series of security questions. It should take no more than ten minutes.

* A valid passport is the only official document you will need when applying.

* You will have to pay an application fee - currently seven euros. Only 18 to 70 year olds must pay.

* It's expected 95 per cent of applications will be straight forward and processed within minutes.

* Applications that require further questions will be processed manually. These should take between 96 hours and two weeks.

* Only a small number of applicants are expected to be invited for interviews.

* Approved applications will be electronically linked to your passport, so you won't need to carry additional ETIAS paperwork.

* Successful applications will be valid for three years.

11. FREE & LOW-COST CAMPING IN EUROPE

Right from when we first started planning our year in a van, we had no intention of spending every night at official campsites. Site fees would gobble up too much of our budget, plus, we had this fanciful idea that we'd go a bit off grid.

To put this in context, we're not exactly Bear Grylls types. Nor is our van one of those hairy 4x4 off-roaders with chunky tyres and a slain wildebeest strapped to the roof rack.

What *we* mean by off-gridding is a finding a reasonably accessible beauty spot up a mountain or by a river or lake, relying on solar panel power for two or three nights, then heading back to civilisation to top up on water or gas and empty our wastewater and unmentionables.

As beginners, the big question for us was, where could we park our campervan, for free where possible, and not get into bother?

The truthful but somewhat vague answer turned out to be… it depends. It depends which country you're in, where you want to overnight and how you behave.

THE BIG WELCOME

Our first big lesson was a positive one. Mainland European countries are, generally, far more welcoming to campervans and motorhomes than the UK.

I'll admit we were sceptical about this before we set off. That was probably the result of being brought up in what can sometimes feel like "Don't do that" "Don't go there" Britain. But our now estranged European cousins seem quite cool about people owning leisure vehicles and encourage their use.

BE CAREFUL WHAT YOU CALL IT

Our second discovery was about terminology. The kind of "camping" I'm talking about here is overnighting in a campervan or motorhome, away from official campsites, self-contained with no electric hook-up or water supply and probably in a remote area. But there's no definitive word for it.

You may come across references to wild camping, free camping, wilding, dry camping, or freedom camping. However, when folks bandy these phrases about, they're often only referring to low-impact camping in tents.

The term "wild camping" causes the greatest confusion. In a few countries, citizens and visitors have a legal right to wild camp. To begin with, we thought this was the best news ever.

But where these rights exist, they are strictly for individuals – not vehicles. Heading off the beaten track in a camper or motorhome packed with every conceivable camping gadget and home-from-home accessory is *not* wild camping in anyone's language. So, sorry folks, but none of us have a legal right to "wild camp" in a vehicle, anywhere.

However, in countries where individuals have that right to access the countryside, we found greater effort seemed to be put into providing designated places for campervan and motorhome stopovers.

These official stopover sites can be at picnic sites, car parks and rest stops where you can usually overnight for free, or a nominal charge. From here onwards, I'm going to call this "informal camping."

The system works on trust. You have the benefit of overnighting in spectacular places at no or little cost, *providing* you follow certain rules or a code of behaviour. It can all go pear-shaped if campers take advantage or turn up at popular locations in vast numbers.

For example, we found lots of "wild" places to stay for free throughout Norway. But on its spectacular Lofoten Islands, there were signs banning any form of camping at many of the must-see tourist hotspots like harbours, beaches, and viewpoints. The locals had clearly had their fill of leisure vehicles.

Even in Scotland (see next chapter), some communities complained of a "motorhome invasion" during the early part of the COVID epidemic. They vented their fury in the press, blaming all types of campers for bad behaviour including "indiscriminate toileting." So, what are the rules?

Specific conditions for parking at these designated spots are usually displayed on signs at each location. Forgive my nagging, but you do need to read them. We ended up with a £60 fine at one overnight stop in Denmark because we mistakenly spent the night in a daytime parking bay. We didn't see the signs when we arrived because they were hidden behind a couple of big motorhomes. Two spaces along and we'd have escaped the fine. Duh!

If there's no English translation on the signs, use the free Google Lens app. That should decipher the local dos and don'ts in any language.

CAMPING CODES & BEHAVING YOURSELF

In countries where individuals have a right to access the countryside, it's usually on the condition that they follow a code of conduct. This is certainly true of Sweden, Norway, and Scotland.

But many other countries also expect a similar standard of behaviour if you're in a leisure vehicle, using remote rural locations or designated stopover sites in more urban areas.

The details of codes vary from country to country, but the gist of them (my interpretation, nothing official) goes something like this:

* Think parking - not camping. No awnings, camping chairs, barbecues, parties or flashing LED flag poles.

* Park for 24 hours - 72 at the most. These are not places to stay for a week.

* Keep well away from residential properties or businesses. Some countries have specific distances. It's 150 metres in Norway.

* Don't cause any kind of obstruction, blocking roads, paths, gateways,

of farm tracks.

* Take extreme care with campfires, only lighting them if local laws allow it or fire pits are provided. European countries with vast acres of forests and woodlands are very sensitive about them being accidentally set ablaze. Some areas have complete bans, others only permit fires at specific times of the year.

* Don't annoy farmers. Keep off cultivated or agricultural land.

* Leave nothing but your footprints. That's no litter, human waste or scorch marks from fires.

* Keep dogs under control. Don't let your four-legged friend chase wildlife and be a paragon of proper poop disposal.

* Basically, be discreet. Keep a low profile and don't push your luck.

URBAN & ROADSIDE STOPOVERS

You don't have to head out into the wilderness to avoid official campsites. Many European countries provide designated spaces where campervans and motorhomes are allowed to park overnight.

Throughout Europe, they're often called "aires" – after the French versions which are generally held up as the gold standard.

They can be beside major roads or motorway routes, in or on the outskirts of towns and sometimes in the smallest villages. Many will have basic facilities for topping up with water or emptying waste, usually for a small fee. The best equipped might even have electric hook-ups and a mini laundrette. Some will have no facilities whatsoever.

And although their number, quality, and the facilities they provide vary enormously, they are at least a place where you know you're allowed to spend the night at little or no cost.

INFORMAL CAMPING

What follows is a quite simple summary of the options for informal camping in the countries we visited. It's not a comprehensive guide, just a top-level insight into each country's attitude to informal camping and what facilities may be available. Informal camping in the UK is a bit complicated, so I'll dig into those delights in the next chapter.

FRANCE

France was not the first country on our itinerary, but it has by far the best network of "aires" for overnight stops. It's estimated there are between four and five thousand of them across the country, near cities, towns, villages, tourist attractions or in the countryside. French aires vary enormously in size, quality, the facilities they offer and what you might pay to use them. You can never book them, they're always available on a first come, first-parked basis. Broadly, there are three main types of aires in France.

French Aires For Overnighting

If you're looking to sleepover, you need an "Aire de camping car." (The French call campervans and motorhomes camping cars.) They're intended for overnight stays and are often provided by local communities or local authorities to attract business.

You'll be able to stay for free, or a small charge. Most have facilities to top up water, empty waste and may even have electrical hook-ups. If you don't pay to stay, there may be a small charge for any services you use.

These types of aires can provide overnight stops in some stunning locations. They have a good reputation, and many travellers cross France just using overnight stops on the "aire de camping car" network.

The easiest way to find them is to type "camping car aire near me" into Google. Or you could use an app like Park4Night or Camper Contact. There's also a detailed book - "Le Guide Officiel Aires de services Camping-car" available on Amazon.

Aire De Service (Service Stop)

There are two further types of French aires which are designed for short, daytime stops only.

An "aire de service" does what it says on le tin. It's a service point where you can top up your drinking water, empty waste and if you're lucky, re-charge your leisure battery. There may also be shops, restaurants, and a hotel at the site. Just to underline it – they're not intended for overnight stays.

Air De Repos (Rest Stop)

You may also come across an "aire de repos" right beside French motorways or major roads. These are rest stops - nothing more. They may have a picnic site and toilets, but there's no guarantee of any other facilities and they're certainly not recommended for overnight stays.

Food Producer Stopovers / Agricamping

An alternative to aires - and a real treat - are overnight stops at foodie businesses in France. The deal is that you can overnight for free, as long as you buy some of their produce, which could be cheese, bread, olives, honey or wine.

Obviously, we chose vineyard for our first producer stopover in France and booked into the Haut-Tellas vineyard at Saint Loubes, North East of Bordeaux.

Proud owner Neil Becede gave us a guided tour of his winery before treating us to a tasting session. Neil gave up a job in engineering to look after his family vineyard, and his passion for his products is infectious.

After a thoroughly enjoyable drink and a really interesting chat about the wine-making process, we bought four bottles from Neil's collection of organic reds and retired to the van which was parked beside a field full of vines. This superb visit cost us just under 50 euros for superb local wines - and absolutely nothing for the overnight.

We found Haut-Tellas through Park4Night, but over 2000 French food businesses, including Neil's, are involved in *France Passion*. You'll need a current guide book (€30 euros) and the membership card supplied with it to take part. Details of how the scheme works can be found on its website:

https://www.france-passion.com/en/motorhomers/how-it-works

The only part of France where we struggled to find aires, day parking for our camper was on the French Riviera coast. Even official campsites seemed few and far between. Perhaps the area prefers a different kind of tourist. You will find places to overnight, but don't expect it to be as easier as pretty much everywhere else in France.

THE NETHERLANDS

To be fair, we passed through The Netherlands rather quickly on our journeys to and from Scandinavia, so didn't explore it fully. But we were aware that the Dutch don't tolerate off-grid camping and won't hesitate to fine you up to 500 euros – each - if they catch you doing it.

Not wanting to incur anyone's wrath in the first country we drove through, we opted to play safe and stayed in two official campsites.

Until recently, you could have got away with "pole camping" in The Netherlands. This scheme, instigated by the Dutch forestry commission, allowed campers and motorhomes to overnight at some remote spots where camping rules were pinned to a pole stuck in the ground. However, during COVID, pole camping was banned throughout The Netherlands and as I write this, remains so.

The Dutch do, however, provide some roadside "aires" for overnight stops. They're few and far between and less well equipped than those in France. Many have no facilities but are at least a possibility for self-contained campers or motorhomes if there's one along your route.

In a densely populated country like The Netherlands, parking in cities is challenging for campers and motorhomes. However, designated camper parking – some of it free – may be found on the outskirts.

We used the invaluable Park4Night app to find a canal-side spot a 25-minute walk from the centre of Delft and a beautiful location close to giant windmills at Schiedam - a short metro ride from the centre of Rotterdam. The Schiedam site had two overnight parking spaces for motorhomes when we visited, though they were the exception rather than the rule.

GERMANY

"Wild camping" is illegal in Germany, but overnight parking is not. The Germans provide over 3,600 "Stellplatz" – their name for "aires". These official stopover sites for campervans and motorhomes are usually provided by local communities. You can find them in the countryside or towns and cities. They'll either be free or charge a modest fee. Sometimes, you just pay for any services you use.

Stellplatz

Our first encounter with a Stellplatz was in the famous Pied Piper rat-catcher's town of Hamelin. It was in a light industrial area and not the prettiest place we'd ever seen. But it did offer drinking water and chemical toilet facilities. Signs at each Stellplatz will explain its specific rules and charges.

Had we been staying the night, we could have hooked up to an electricity supply, for a fee. But we weren't. It was early in our expedition, and being honest, we were a bit chicken at that stage; still roosting in official campsites, building up our courage to overnight in glorified parking lots.

We did, however, summon up enough bottle to use the Hamelin Stellplatz for day parking. It was a treat to find parking spaces big enough for our van.

We also met some fellow Brits there, a middle-aged couple who had travelled the length and breadth of Europe for years, always staying in Stellplatz - or their equivalents. Much encouraged, we paid the seven-euro day parking fee and took a very enjoyable 30-minute walk along the River Weser to the historic city centre to catch a rat or two.

Travelling through Germany, you may come across other facilities which allow camper and motorhome stopovers.

Autohofs

Autohofs are privately-run overnight parking areas. They're usually a short distance off major roads, often close to junctions. There'll be a fee to use them, but they're usually secure with fences, security cameras and facilities.

You might be offered a refund or discount on your overnight fee if you use any shops, restaurants, or fuel stations at these sites. The Autohofs are not exclusively for campervans and motorhomes. They're popular with lorry drivers too.

Rastattes

Rastattes (rest stops) are parking areas that are found right beside Germany's autobahns or main roads. Parking is usually free, but you're likely to be charged to use facilities, if there are any. These are not intended or recommended for overnight stays. There are enough horror stories about excessive noise, lack of security and undesirables gathering at rastattes to suggest they should only be used for overnighting in an emergency.

SWEDEN

Like other Scandinavian countries, the Swedes work from the basic premise that the land belongs to everyone. Therefore, it has "Allemanstratten" - roughly translated as every man's right to roam.

Citizens and visitors can visit, explore, hike, forage, and camp (in tents), almost anywhere in the countryside. Sweden is a good example of where these rights apply to individuals – not vehicles – and only then if they follow one of those codes of conduct that I mentioned earlier.

However, the spirit if not the law of Allemenstratten does help the campervan and motorhome community. The country provides many picnic spots, car parks and rest spots where you are allowed to park your leisure vehicle for the night. Once again, we found them using the Park4Night app and the majority were free.

It's worth noting that the Swedish Island of Gotland in the Baltic Sea is an exception. It introduced its own rules banning campervans motorhome overnights in any public places. Here, you must use official campsites.

Flatpack Parking

When we were visiting towns and cities in Sweden, we were surprised but delighted to discover that we were allowed to spend the night in the car parks at branches of IKEA. I know! It sounds ridiculous.

The iconic meatball maestros positively encourage campervan and motorhome parking in their home country. While no facilities are provided, you do have access to the store's restaurants and toilets during opening hours.

We stayed in three IKEA car parks during our Scandinavian travels. Sure, they weren't beauty spots, but they felt safe, were well lit and provided much appreciated, free stop-offs along our route. The IKEA outside Bergen in Norway even had a free shuttle bus into the city.

You can also stay in the car park at the official IKEA Museum in Almhult. And that museum (much to the surprise of our mates) is well worth a visit - as you'll discover in future books. Check on those on my blog: vanlifevirgins.com.

FINLAND

We spent only a few hours in Finland, skirting just inside its border as we crossed from the North of Sweden into Norway. Norwegians have something like the Swede's "right to roam," but once again, this applies to individuals, not vehicles. That said, you're allowed to park in designated picnic spots and car parks which you can find using apps like Park4Night.

You may also get away with overnight parking at more remote sites, providing you don't drive off-road and keep at least 150 metres away from the nearest house of hut.

Individual communities in Finland have the power to ban overnight stops for motorhomes and campers in their areas, so it's important to read any signs. The Fins also discourage the lighting of campfires anywhere but in designated fire pits.

NORWAY

There's only one way to put this. We could not have afforded to explore Norway if we'd not been able to overnight in free parking spots, picnic areas and rest areas.

We found Norway a staggeringly expensive country. Basic food and provisions put pressure on our daily budgets. Here's a mind-boggling example: two pints of run-of-the-mill lager in Oslo's tourist hotspot harbour… £24.

And while diesel didn't seem significantly more expensive than fuel back home, the huge distances we covered in this exceptionally long country racked up our travel costs. Campsite costs on top of all this would have broken the bank.

Once again, good old Park4Night helped us find overnight locations. And just like in Sweden, accessing the countryside is on condition that you follow the code of conduct I outlined earlier.

Some of our overnight locations were truly spectacular. One of our favourites was at an abandoned ferry terminal in Saeterbukta Bay on the Lofoten Islands. We parked our van on the disused jetty and had spectacular views up and down the Fjord, saw shoals of fish circling whirlpool-like in the crystal-clear waters and spiky sea urchins clinging to the rocks at the water's edge. Idyllic.

However, it was a different story at the more popular tourist hot spots on the Lofotens. We found "No Camping" signs all over the fishing village of Henningsvaer – home of the much-photographed football stadium that sticks out into the sea on its own headland. It was the same story when we tried visiting Haukland beach, allegedly one of the most beautiful beaches in Europe.

We don't mind paying to stay at official campsites close to these must-see destinations. I'm just making the point that you can't rely on being able to find free overnight parking everywhere – even in Norway.

DENMARK

Denmark has that Scandinavian freedom to roam, but with the brakes slightly on. It's more densely populated and its landscape more cultivated than Sweden and Norway.

That said, overnight camping is tolerated in laybys – or "Rasteplads" – providing you go into discrete mode. Signs will alert you if overnighting is not allowed. You'll probably be able to stay in designated parking spots or picnic spots, particularly on the coast. And let's face it, Denmark has a lot of coast. There's even a scheme called "Bondegårdscamping" – where some farmers allow overnight stays on their farms. See: https://bondegaardsferie.dk/en/

SPAIN

We weren't expecting much from "Aparcamientos autocaravans" - the Spanish equivalent of aires. Travel bloggers had warned they were few and far between, and where they did exist, had poor or no facilities - and still might charge as much as official campsites.

In reality, we were pleasantly surprised. With an estimated 500 aires across the whole of Spain, they are harder to find than in France, but we came across charming examples in mountain villages - complete with facilities. Plus, big cities like Seville have enormous parking grounds for campers within half an hour's walk of the city centre.

Municipal Aires

The Spanish aires that do exist are usually provided by local councils, often on the outskirts of towns or in a section of a public or supermarket car park. These municipal aires are available on a first come, first-can-stay basis. They may be free or, charge a small fee.

As per everywhere, the specific rules for stopovers will vary from site to site, but they'll be broadly in line with those elsewhere in Europe, encouraging you to treat your stay as parking, not camping. There are reports that some Spanish towns take this further than most, not allowing people to sit or eat outside their vans, even in the hottest weather.

Privately run Aires

Spain also has some privately-run aires where the rules are more relaxed. They're more like basic campsites where you'll be able to book in advance and you'll be charged a fee. Some are close to major tourist attractions. Others are at local businesses, like vineyards, which provide the overnight facilities to attract customers. They often offer that familiar deal where you can stay for free, providing you buy some of their product.

You can find over two hundred Spanish businesses involved in the scheme at: https://espana-discovery.es/

Service Points

There are campervan and motorhome service points on Spanish motorways, but again, far fewer than in France. These may charge for topping up with water and emptying waste and are not designed for overnight stays.

ITALY

Before we set off, I'd read mixed reviews about campervanning in Italy and was a little nervous about what we'd find. Based entirely on our five-week stint in Italy, all I can say is it was nowhere near as difficult as I feared.

Sostas

Italian aires, or "Sostas" as they're called, take many forms and they are much harder to find than in France. However, they do exist. We had fantastic stopovers in vineyards with electricity and superb showers - for a fee. We stayed at several, picturesque, village-run Sostas with basic facilities and paid nothing.

When it came to visiting cities like Venice, Florence, Rome - and tourist hotspots like Pompei and the Amalfi Coast - we discovered formal campsites were our only option. And there weren't many of those to choose from.

They often had the word Sosta" in their names, but in the UK would be considered fully-fledged campsites. Ours were all some distance from city centres or major attractions, so we left the van at the campsite and used public transport - including a dilapidated 1920s tram to visit Rome and an occasionally terrifying descent down a mountain road on a bus to Amalfi. All adds to the fun.

The best value Sosta we discovered was in Ruvo di Puglia (Via Scarlatti) not far from Bari. We wondered why it had such good facilities at such a reasonable price - then discovered it was run by the local campervan and motorhome club.

Informal Camping

Some online articles stress that "wild camping" is generally prohibited across Italy – with great variation in the way individual localities interpret and enforce the rules.

There are warnings that you're most likely to upset the authorities if you camp in the wrong place near tourist attractions on the coast. Fines range from 100 to 500 euros.

Some travellers report there's loophole that allows you to park anywhere if you can convince the authorities you were too tired to continue driving and needed to rest. But be warned, you could still be fined if your parked up vehicle protrudes over the lines of a designated parking space.

You may even get into trouble for extending the "perimeter" of your vehicle too. Apparently, this includes winding out your awning or - if you encounter a particularly zealous Italian policeman - opening a side window on your camper or motorhome.

That said, some seasoned travel bloggers knock all this on the head claiming they've managed to spend eighty per cent of their Italian trips overnight parking off gird without any problems. Which is true? All I can say is we didn't encounter any difficulties, although we were in Italy during March and the places we visited were pretty quiet. It may be a different story in the height of summer.

Service Points

Supermarkets and garages across Italy may provide services for topping up drinking water. In the North, you have a good chance of finding waste disposal facilities too. In contrast, you may struggle to find somewhere to empty grey and toilet waste in the South of the country, unless you check in to a formal campsite.

I've read one report that fines for draining water in unauthorised places can be as much as 335 euros.

Agricamping

Agricamping sounds a bit more consistent. As in France, Spain and Denmark, farmers and other local food and drink businesses, welcome campervans, and motorhomes. They're often in beautiful rural settings – with opportunities for walking and trekking. Your stay may be free if you eat, drink, or buy some of your host's products. We stayed at two "agri-sostas" in Italy and had a superb welcome at both. Find out more about the Italian Agricamping network at: https://www.ariapp.it

ALBANIA

We spent nearly three months in Albania. There's no equivalent of "aires" because they're not needed. There appear to be no specific rules against informal camping. The country's vast amount of wild, unpopulated countryside and stunning mountain regions offer lots of scope for overnight stops. Just don't stay on any obviously private land or in Albania's national parks or nature reserves. The authorities are a little touchy about that.

In reality, we didn't "informal camp" as much as you'd imagine because the official campsites were so inexpensive - if a little rudimentary.

MONTENEGRO

Officially, overnighting in vehicles is a no no in Montenegro.

CROATIA

Off-grid camping in Croatia is strictly forbidden. Get caught and you could be stung with a 400 Euro fine. We stuck to official campsites on our short trip through Croatia, which were noticeably more expensive than those in surrounding countries.

SLOVENIA

Informal camping is not allowed in Slovenia either. It's a 500 Euro fine if you get caught overnighting off grid. Though there are said to be 130 to 150 designated camper stopovers throughout the country.

We had a short run through Slovenia at the start of our journey home, but managed to found one of the best value "aires" on our entire trip. The camper stop just outside Stari Trg Pri Lozu was provided by the local community. It was clean, modern, had useful maps of local attractions, fresh water, waste disposal, wi-fi and even electricity for free.

AUSTRIA

The precise rules for overnight camping vary from state to state. But the general rule is you can't do it unless you the have the express permission of a landowner. Fines can be up to 500 euros.

Official campsites can be a little expensive by UK standards - but considerably cheaper than a fine of up to 14,000 euros that I've read you could be clobbered with if you try overnighting in a national park, nature reserve or other protected area.

SWITZERLAND

Switzerland is a bit of a mixed bag when it comes to informal camping. Each area has its own rules, so it's a case of making sure you read any signs.

If you are allowed to overnight in a car park, the rules are like those in many countries. Make sure you're in a designated space and think parking, not camping. That means no awnings, tables, chairs or barbeques outside your camper or motorhome, and moving on the next morning.

12. FREE & LOW-COST CAMPING IN THE UK

The most challenging leg of our year-long trip around Europe was without doubt our enforced return to the UK.

We'd spent an exciting July, August and September exploring Sweden, Norway, and Denmark. In a pre-Brexit world, we would have wrapped up Scandinavia and followed the Autumn sunshine to Southern Spain. But as October approached, we had used up the "90 days in any 180 days" we post-Brexit Brits are allowed to stay in Schengen Zone countries. Simply, we had to get out.

I've explained the travel restrictions we now face as non-EU citizens in chapter ten, so won't moan on about them again. For us, the rules meant we couldn't enter another Schengen Area country for a further 90 days, so it made the most sense to return home to the good old UK which never has been and probably never will be in the Schengen Zone.

Remember, we couldn't go home home. We'd rented out our flat for a year to fund our big trip. There was someone living in it. So, we had to spend October, November, and December, in the UK, in our van and try to live within our daily rent-from-the-flat budget.

There were some positive reasons to be back in Blighty. Steve's daughter was getting married, my youngest was due to have a baby and I had a big birthday approaching. So that was three days sorted. It was the remaining eighty-seven that were going to be the challenge.

Don't get me wrong, we both love the UK. Even after all our many travels, I'm still astounded by the variety of landscapes and stunning places we can explore on our relatively small nation.

I convinced myself we could count down the days until we could legally return to Europe by visiting UK locations and attractions that had been on our radars for years, but we'd never managed to visit.

However, the challenge was finding free camping spots to balance our budget. The UK does *not* share our continental cousins' tolerance of informal camping in motorhomes and campers.

ENGLAND AND WALES

I've mentioned that Norway and Sweden have a very generous approach to giving people access to the countryside. They're big, sparsely populated countries and have a fundamental belief that, in spirit at least, nature belongs to everyone.

In England and Wales, it's the complete opposite. Our islands are densely populated, and virtually every square inch of them belongs to someone. The upshot is that, legally, you cannot overnight with a camper or motorhome on any piece of land in the UK unless you have the landowner's permission. If you don't have permission, it's trespassing.

In practice, there are places where landowners have explicitly given you permission to camp, such as where signs clearly state camping is allowed in a car park. Plus, there are other locations where overnight parking (note, I'm avoiding the word camping) is tolerated, providing you're discreet and behave respectfully.

But how do you find these places? We discovered nearly all our free overnight parks using the Park4Night app. Other apps and websites are available as you'll see in Appendix 1. But remember, just because a location is listed on an app or in a book of guide, there is no 100% guarantee you have permission to be there. You must be careful.

CAMPING LAWS IN ENGLAND AND WALES

Once again, I need to remind you that passing Essential Law for Journalists when I was an 18-year-old trainee newspaper reporter does not make me a lawyer. Therefore, not a single word you read in this book should be taken as legal advice.

The reason I'm disclaiming yet again is because the subject of where you can overnight in your campervan and motorhome is complicated. Several different laws can come into play, depending on the circumstances.

A 200-year-old vagrancy act was often quoted as the reason wild camping was not allowed in England and Wales. It was originally introduced to clear the streets of destitute soldiers after the Napoleonic Wars, and its punishments for sleeping outdoors – no matter what the reason – could include being sent to a "house of correction" for a year. Unpleasant.

But as we've discovered, overnighting in motorhomes and campervans is not wild camping, this antiquated piece of legislation was never really our concern. What we must contend with is the civil offence of trespassing.

You'll be trespassing if you take a leisure vehicle onto any land in England and Wales without the landowner's permission. It's usually a civil offence, so you won't be arrested or get a criminal record, providing you move on promptly should the landowner or police ask you to. It could get hairier if you refuse to move on or cause a nuisance.

How much hairier is spelt out in the recent Police, Crime, Sentencing and Courts Act (2022). Should you ever lose the will to live, you can read it in full at: https://www.legislation.gov.uk/ukpga/2022/32

Here's what I have taken home from the Act's section on "Unauthorised Encampments - residing on land without consent in or with a vehicle." By the way, a temporary visit in a campervan, motorhome or caravan is considered "residing" as far as this piece of legislation is concerned.

The trouble will start if you have taken a vehicle onto land without permission and don't leave "as soon as reasonably practicable" after being requested to do so. That request can come from the landowner, someone representing them or a police officer. Respond politely, leave quickly and you should hear no more about it.

However, if you leave as requested and then return, you could be in trouble. It could also become a criminal matter if you cause considerable damage or disruption while you're on the land or do something so offensive you cause someone significant distress. The new law also introduces the possibility that the police could seize your campervan or motorhome while any investigations are conducted.

If you're eventually convicted at a magistrate's court, you could be jailed for up to three months, or fined up to £2,500.

COUNCIL CAR PARKS

Many public car parks are owned by local councils which, in some matters, are allowed to be a law unto themselves. They're able to make local Traffic Regulation Orders (TROs) and apply rules and restrictions to specific roads or car parks in their patch.

This can be a good thing. One of our favourite council car parks (yes, we have such things) is in the centre of Skipton at the edge of the Yorkshire Dales, close to the town's picturesque canal basin. Here, the enlightened Craven District Council has allocated five large parking bays specially for motorhomes. It's not free to stay - £5 when we last visited - but at least it's clear that overnighting is allowed. As with most council car parks, the rules, regulations and charges are displayed very clearly on signs.

TROs can also be used for the opposite effect, banning any form of overnight stays, cooking, or sleeping in vehicles. Again, all the rules will be spelt out very clearly on signs.

Sometimes, councils offer stopover spaces on an experimental basis. Since 2017, another of our favourite local towns, Helmsley on the North York Moors, allowed up to six campers or motorhomes to stay for free in its Cleveland Way car park. On our most recent visit, we were surprised to see height barriers had been erected, accompanied by signs saying no sleeping in vehicles was allowed.

It turns out local people had complained about the lighting of fires and "irresponsible waste disposal" in the car park when staycations exploded during the early phase of the COVID pandemic. Abuse it and lose it… as they say.

PRIVATE CAR PARKS

Can you overnight in a privately owned car park such as an NCP? Well, you could, (cue the stuck record!), providing you have the landowner's permission.

We've visited a Morrisons car park near Peterborough which , at the time of our visit, allowed stopovers for campervans and motorhomes. But it is a bit of an exception. Don't assume all Morrisons will allow you to park for the night, it's entirely down to an individual store's discretion. It may be worth enquiring at customer services.

Some private companies, hotels, vineyards, antique centres, or sporting venues such as golf clubs might let you park free for the night too. Once again, you'll need their express permission to do so. There are specific apps and publications like https://www.britstops.com/ to help you find them in the UK.

PUB CAR PARKS

An increasingly popular opportunity for stopovers is pub car parks.

Some publicans encourage overnight stays because it's good for their business. The deal is much like those at rural foodie and winey businesses in Europe. You can stay for free, providing you have a meal and a few drinks in the pub. No great hardship - especially if you're looking for somewhere to eat out anyway.

It's unlikely there'll be any camping facilities, so as with the other types of overnight parking listed above, pub stopovers are only suitable for self-contained campervans and motorhomes. It's also likely that there will only be one or two spaces available on a first-come, first-served basis.

We managed to get a free space in the Wheatsheaf pub car park in the centre of Corbridge, Northumberland – an ideal starting point for exploring the spectacular Kielder Forest. We checked in on arrival and celebrated our good fortune with friends in the bar, fulfilling our part of the bargain.

While pub stopovers are a great possibility for overnight parking, it can be quite an informal arrangement and property owners are under no obligation to provide the service. It's a good idea to call publicans before you turn up, just to make sure they're still taking part in the pub stopover scheme or that their spaces are not already full.

The services pubs can offer can be restricted by planning laws and The Caravan Sites and Control of Development Act 1960. The legislation can limit the number of vehicles allowed on land, and the number of days that they're allowed to park before landowners are required to obtain an exemption certificate of planning permission.

This red tape is for publicans to worry about, but it does mean the opportunity to stop over at some locations may be far from permanent.

LAYBYS

In your travels around England and Wales, you'll spot some campers and motorhomes parked up for the night in roadside laybys that are usually owned by local councils. And while they're certainly not designated as camping areas, you may get away with overnight parking if you treat area like a rest stop. It's more than likely lorry drivers will be using them to rest up too.

The consensus seems to be that while we have no rights to stopover in English laybys, there's no specific law making it illegal. Though the good old Cravan Sites and Control of Development Act is likely to kick in if laybys are used like caravan sites.

If you do use laybys, it's suggested you arrive late and leave early. Don't put anything outside your van that will make it look as though you're camping. Leave no trace of your visit and if you are asked to move on – do so at once.

INFORMAL CAMPING IN SCOTLAND

Scotland is a hugely popular destination for anyone with a campervan or motorhome, due to its spectacular scenery and reputation for allowing "wild camping."

The scenery won't let you down, but if you're expecting the freedom to park a leisure vehicle in any remote spot you fancy, you'll be disappointed.

As with similar rights in Scandinavian countries, the much-vaunted "freedom to roam" in the Scottish countryside applies solely to individuals, not vehicles. The Land Reform (Scotland) Act of 2003 *does* allow "wild camping" if you're a low-impact, leave-no-trace camper in a tent – but not if you're trundling around the Trossachs, or any part of Scotland for that matter, in a campervan or motorhome. The Act specifically excludes motor vehicles.

That said, we felt we had a distinctly warmer welcome campervanning around Scotland than we did in England. We managed to camp for free, legally we assume, for all but two of the seventeen nights we spent North of the Border. And our trip included the spectacular and popular NC500 route around the Northern tip of this stunning country.

At a local level, councils seem keen to provide designated overnight spaces for campervans and motorhomes - sometimes with facilities.

Nationally, instead of complaining about the boom in leisure vehicles, particularly since COVID, bodies responsible for the countryside have been allowing overnighting in more of their car parks to take pressure of local communities and businesses.

FORESTRY AND LAND SCOTLAND (FLS)

We were grateful to benefit from the "Stay the Night" scheme run by Forestry and Land Scotland (FLS). FLS has allowed self-contained campervan and motorhomes to stay for single nights in 37 of its car parks from April to October. Stays can be from 6pm to 10am, with no return visit for 48 hours, usually for free or a small charge.

The scheme was set up in the aftermath of COVID to reduce pressure on tourism "honey pots." And while Forestry bosses have been positive about the scheme, it remains a trial and is continually evaluated. Always check out when and where it is running at: https://forestryandland.gov.scot/stay-the-night

THE HIGHLAND COUNCIL

The council which covers The Highlands was running a similar trial scheme when we headed north to tackle the NC500.

It also allowed single night stays for campers and motorhomes in designated bays at 12 of its existing car parks. 10pm to 8am stays cost £10 per stay with no return within 72 hours. As usual, the emphasis is on parking, not camping - so no awnings, camping chairs of campfires allowed.

The car parks included in the scheme for the 2022 season were:

* Torvean - Inverness

* Nairn Harbour

* Dunnet Head, Dunnet Seadrift, Noss Head & Reiss Beach - Caithness

* Riverside - Wick

* Durness Village & Golspie Shore - Sutherland

* Ullapool Latheron, Gairloch Harbour, Little Gruinard Beach - Wester Ross

As I write this, the trial is being evaluated, so check https://www.highland.gov.uk/ and search "motorhomes" to find the latest situation.

Being English, we at once thought we'd done something wrong when a Highland Council ranger pulled his van up beside ours when we'd parked in the tiny harbour at Lybster, just south of Wick, to take some photos.

The ranger turned out to be very friendly and helpful. He gave us a shiny leaflet *Enjoying the Highlands in your Motorhome or Campervan*, plus some top tips on places to visit that were off the usual tourist trail. How un-English was that!

The ranger's booklet confirmed that, under the Road Traffic Act 1998, campervans and motorhomes were allowed to park overnight in formal, roadside laybys in Scotland - providing all activity is within the vehicle. This is what we had suspected, but it was re-assuring to have it confirmed in black and white.

Our introduction to Highland scenery was on our trek north through the Cairngorms National Park, following the "Snow Road" which runs from Blairgowrie, passing by Balmoral and onwards to Grantown on Spey.

The National Park produces a detailed map listing all the facilities that are available for people travelling in campers and motorhomes – including formal campsites, showers, laundrettes, public toilets, black and grey waste disposal sites, as well as overnight parking. See the latest version of the map at: https://www.visitcairngorms.com/wp-content/uploads/2021/06/Campervan-Map-Optimised.pdf

NATURE SCOT

One of the best informal overnight stops we had was in the car park at the Muir of Dinnet Nature Reserve Visitor Centre, near Aboyne. It's run by Nature Scot, formerly known as Scottish Natural Heritage.

This centre provides drinking water, chemical waste disposal, toilets and hot water, in return for a voluntary donation. And the real bonus - a selection of nature trails through the reserve that all start at the visitor centre.

Nature Scott has no fixed policy for overnight stays at its reserves, and does not usually provide facilities, so it's a case of checking signage at individual car parks.

SCOTTISH ACCESS CODE

Signs at most designated overnight parking spots in Scotland made it clear that we were being allowed to park, not camp. And if we stayed, it was on condition that we followed the gist of the Scottish Access Code.

Technically, the code is aimed at people who camp in tents, but folks in campers and motorhomes can avoid a lot of trouble if they follow the same rules. Its general points are remarkably like the codes used in Scandinavia:

* Keep away from houses, agricultural land, businesses and activities like tree-felling and harvesting

*Don't do anything that could annoy or alarm people, especially at night.

* Don't disturb nature and don't leave litter

* Keep control of your dog, especially near livestock and during the bird nesting season. Always pick up after your pooch.

And while motor vehicles have no access rights, the code says people driving into the countryside should:

* Not cause obstructions

* Never make it difficult for others to use roads or tracks

* Try not to damage verges, and

* Always use a car park if there is one nearby

NOT SO INFORMAL CAMPING – LOCH LOMOND & THE TROSSACHS

While general camping freedoms can be enjoyed throughout Scotland, a few particularly popular areas have opted out and imposed restrictions.

We came across our first "Camping Zone" signs when we pulled into a car park on the banks of Loch Lomond one dismal Saturday afternoon in late October.

As it turned out, the local restrictions didn't apply to us because we'd arrived after the end of the main season. But if we'd wanted to stay at any time from March 1st to September 30th, we would have needed a permit. So, if you are thinking of visiting the Loch Lomond and The Trossachs National Park during that period, you'll need to plan ahead.

The National Park Authority introduced camping restrictions in 2017 because of fears that certain areas were under threat from the sheer number of visitors. The whole park isn't in a "permit area," just certain hotspots which come under the most pressure. The easiest way to check which precise locations are affected – and buy permits - is to visit the national park's permit website:

https://www.lochlomond-trossachs.org/things-to-do/camping/get-a-permit/

You must apply for permits, online, in advance. If you leave it until the last minute, you might not get one. There are a limited number of permits issued each day for campers and motorhomes.

Permits cost £4 per vehicle, per day. They allow you to park in your selected permit area, but do not guarantee a specific parking spot. You'll be expected to arrive after 1pm and leave the next day before 11am. And just because you've paid, don't expect any facilities. Remember, you're paying for something close to a "wild camping" experience.

If you can't get a permit, the National Park provides campsites at Loch Chon, Loch Achray and Inchcailloch. These are only open for the main season.

I appreciate all this malarkey is designed to protect the countryside. That's what National Parks do. But there's no doubt it all feels a bit of a faff compared to the ease and informality of camping elsewhere in Scotland. I'm glad we rolled up at Loch Lomond out of season.

NORTHERN IRELAND / IRELAND

We didn't make it to Northern Ireland, or Ireland, on our big trip but it's my understanding that "wild camping" in motorhomes is illegal in both jurisdictions unless you have the landowner's permission.

The Northern Ireland Forestry Commission has issued permits that allow leisure vehicles to overnight at some of its forest locations. These sites usually have good facilities - including electric hook-ups. You'll find more details at:

https;//www.nidirect.gov.uk/services/tollymore-forest-park-camping-touring-online-booking

Informal stopover sites exist in NI and Ireland. For help finding them, consider becoming a member of Safe Nights Ireland (SNI). This organisation lists over 350 safe sites for overnight parking - rural locations as well as in cities including Dublin, where you'll pay a small fee. Membership charges are 15 euros a year. www.safenightsireland.com

The website UK Motorhomes includes officially recognised overnight camping spots in Ireland, as well as the UK.

Also , Total Motorhomes Ireland (TMI) is a popular Facebook group offers advice and useful maps.

13. ROAD TOLLS IN EUROPE

When it comes to road tolls – paying fees to drive along a specific section of road in campervans, motorhomes, or any other vehicle – we Brits are somewhat out of step with most of our neighbours in Europe. Now there's a surprise.

We don't do road tolls - apart from that stretch of the M6 in the Midlands which is a bit of an anomaly. We'll reluctantly cough up cash to cross over some bridges, or travel through tunnels, but providing we've paid our road tax, we consider it a basic human right to trundle along anything from a B-road to a motorway toll free.

That's why it comes as a shock when we're confronted with kilometre after kilometre or toll roads in Europe.

The general assumption is that toll roads justify the fees because they're faster and in much better condition than their non-toll alternatives.

In our experience, this stacks up - apart from in France. This may just be due to the routes we took, but we travelled from Calais to Northern Spain without going on a single toll road - and the French A roads and motorways were superb. I can't grasp why the French have any toll roads when their free alternatives are so good.

In Italy, however, the difference is monumental. We ended up doing most of our Italian touring on toll roads because the rest of the country's rural and urban roads were in such an appalling condition. That sounds a bit general - but 14,000 miles into our trip, they were undoubtedly the worst road surfaces we have encountered (until we left the main roads in Albania).

Enough of the road rage. The general guide that follows is as exact as I can make it at the time of writing. Bear in mind that countries are continually changing their road toll policies, prices, and methods of payment. So, always check on the latest situation in the country you intend to visit before your travel. Web links for specific countries are includes, where available.

NO ROAD TOLL COUNTRIES

The UK is not entirely alone in having few toll roads. The countries listed below are pretty much road toll free, though you may still be charged to use certain bridges or tunnels.

* Albania (apart from the A1 Rruga e Kombit motorway)

* Andora (Envalira Tunnel charge only)

* Belgium

* Cyprus

* Denmark (tolls on several major bridges)

* Estonia (unless over 3.5 tonnes)

* Finland

* Germany

* Iceland (apart from one tunnel)

* Kosovo

* Liechtenstein (Tolls for vehicles over 12 tonnes)

* Lithuania (Vehicles over 3.5 tonnes need vignette - see below)

* Luxembourg (apart from vehicles over 12 tonnes)

* Malta

* Monaco

* Montenegro (Sozina Tunnel only - though tolls may soon be introduced on A1 motorway)

* The Netherlands (tolls on Westerschelde and Kil Tunnels)

* Sweden (Tolls on Oresund, Svinesund, Motala & Sundsvalls bridges

* Ukraine.

TRADITIONAL ROAD TOLLS

Many countries that charge for driving on sections of roads have what we might call traditional-type tolls. These are where you only pay for the distance of toll road you drive on.

In the countries listed below, you have the option of collecting a ticket from a toll booth when you enter the tolled section and present your ticket at a pay booth just before you leave. The fee is based on the distance you've travelled on the tolled section.

When you approach a payment toll, there'll often be a choice of lanes to drive through, depending on how you intend to pay. You can still pay by cash at some booths, but that means carrying a shed load of coins with you. Plus, you're unlikely to get a receipt for cash payments.

Choosing to pay by card is easier and guarantees you have a record of the payment. That may come in useful if you're ever challenged.

COUNTRIES WITH PAY AS YOU GO TOLLS

* Croatia - see www.hac.hr

* France - see www.autoroutes.fr

* Greece

* Ireland - some parts of motorways, tunnels and bridges

* Italy - www.autostrada.it

* Latvia - for vehicles over three tonnes

* Norway - https://www.autopass.no/en/

* Poland

* Portugal - Some tolls are autopay only. See http://www.visitportugal.com/en. Portugal also offers a pre-paid toll cars for foreign vehicles.

* Ireland - M50 toll is autopay only. See https://www.eflow.ie/

* Spain - www.autopistas.com

AUTOPAY ACCOUNTS

An increasingly popular method of paying traditional road tolls is to drive through the "Auto pay" lane. This is only possible if you have pre-registered for an "autopay" account that covers the country you're driving in.

To setup an account, you'll need to give your vehicle registration number, so it's recognised by cameras at the toll booths. You'll also be asked for vehicle details, including its fuel type as toll rates may vary depending on CO_2 emissions. Giving your bank account details will allow payments to be taken automatically.

In some countries, like France, you can choose between several different companies that run "autopay" services. We were put off using any of the French versions after reading several online reviews. Some British users complain that accounts are difficult to set up and even more challenging when things go wrong because customer services tended to be only in French.

However, we had no problems whatsoever using the automated "EPass24" system in Norway – a country with many stretches of what seemed to us almost empty tolled roads. It worked very efficiently and even processed payments for us using some ferries. There's are so many Fjords in Norway, ferry crossings are considered part of the country's road network.

The only downside is that payments aren't processed as you drive along, so you don't know how much you're spending day to day. The system adds up all your tolls for one month and takes a single payment from your bank towards the end of the following month. For what it's worth, a full month of driving around Norway cost us £86 in road and (some) ferry tolls. Though we did do a lot of driving.

PRE-PAID TOLLS & VIGNETTES

Some countries are now extracting toll road fees from you in a different way – with a pre-paid "vignette." These are a sticker that you buy and mount in your windscreen before you travel.

You pay a flat rate for the number of days you need to travel on the road network. It seems common for countries who use this pay-in-advance system to offer drivers three main options for vignettes that cover:

* Seven to ten days

* One or two months or

* One year

You can usually buy vignettes at or close to border crossings, or from petrol stations and convenience stores in adjacent countries. It's important to buy a vignette before you drive on the road network it covers.

And another word of warning, make sure you follow the instructions on the back of a vignette on where to stick it! If roadside cameras can't read a windscreen vignette, you could end up with a fine. It's also a clever idea to keep your counterfoil copy just in case you should ever need to prove you had a vignette.

Vignettes are **compulsory** for driving in the following countries:

* Austria - (for national motorways and dual carriageways. www.asfinag.at. We bought ours at a filling station in Slovenia, just before we crossed the border into Austria. Many Austrian tunnels have additional tolls.

* Bulgaria - (whole road network). http://www.highwaymaps.eu/bulgaria

* Czech Republic - https://edalnice.cz/en/index.html#validation

* Estonia - for vehicles over 3.5 tonnes. https://teetasu.ee

* Hungary - for vehicles up to 7.5 tonnes. https://ematrica.nemzetiutdij.hu/en/log-in

* Lithuania - mostly for goods vehicles and those carrying more than eight passengers.

* Moldova

* Romania - compulsory on all main roads outside cities and towns.

* Slovakia

* Slovenia - for vehicles under 3.5 tonnes. Heavier vehicles need to register for a Darsgo electronic tag. www.darsgo.si

* Switzerland - only an annual vignette is available for around 40 euros. www.myswitzerland.com. We spent only two days driving through Switzerland on our way home. We spent only two days travelling through Switzerland on our way home, making our Swiss vignette the worst value of any road toll we paid on our 21,000 mile adventure.

POLUTION & CONGESTION CHARGES

While these are not road tolls as such, you may need to pay extra to enter major cities throughout Europe – particularly if your campervan or motorhome isn't that impressive in the emissions department.

The drive to save the planet means new congestion zones and clean air zones are being introduced everywhere and at speed. Whether you'll pay will depend entirely on local rules and how much your vehicle pollutes.

For example, I had to cough up £12 a day to enter London's Ultra Low Emissions Zone in our good old 2016 plate VW T6 camper. However, our current camper Cliff meets Euro 6 emissions standards and can pass through ULEZ toll free.

If you insist on driving your camper or motorhome into any European city, it's important to check whether you need to pay either congestion or clean air charges, and where possible pay online, in advance - or at least register your vehicle if you're required to.

In reality, we found it really difficult to work out what the rules are.

In Madrid, for example, the city's emission zone and accompanying website is focused on residents, not tourists. We read conflicting information on whether foreign vehicles were even included in the scheme. Not helpful when you're already en route to the city centre.

Plus, if you don't know a city, it's hard to work out where a zone begins on the ground. After a couple of unexpected roadsign warnings that we were about to enter a restricted zone, we did a U-turn and headed back to the outskirts, parked up, and took the Metro into the city centre.

The best piece of advice I can give you, based entirely on our experience, is don't attempt to take a campervan or motorhome into cities at all. Apart from potential charges, it can be really challenging to find big enough parking spaces in these congested areas.

Our visits to Stockholm, Gothenburg, Oslo, Copenhagen, Florence, Rome, Naples, Tirana and Salzburg were trouble free, because we always parked our van on the outskirts, and used their superb public transport systems to travel into the heart of each city. The Stockholm metro system is a tourist attraction in its own right – but that's for a later book. Look out for those more detailed journals of our travels at Vanlifevirgins.com.

14. LIVING IN A BOX

I hope your dream campervan or motorhome trip is now feeling more doable. Of course, you'll need to research your own adventure in specific detail, but at least this book has given you a checklist of topics to think through and a few pointers based on our experience. What I haven't covered is what an extended road trip does to your head.

I wouldn't be writing this book if I didn't one hundred percent recommend a grown-up gap year in a van. But I'm not suggesting it's all plain sailing after you watch everything that's familiar in your life disappear in your rear-view mirror.

The terrific freedom vanlife gives you comes with a few challenges. You may have none – but here are some of mine.

THE COURAGE TO DO IT

After creating the space in your life for a big trip and working out how to fund it, making the decision to actually go ahead is still a big hurdle.

Our leap of faith was nothing compared to folks who sell up everything and commit to permanent life on the road. Our trip was always intended to be a big break – a chance to reset. We always planned to return home after twelve months, but even so, it was a big deal.

Everyone's reasons for sampling van life are different. Like all NHS workers, Steve had been pushed to his limits during the COVID pandemic. And while I didn't face challenges on the level he did, my work producing videos for the NHS started drying up.

Plus, we were about to get married. So, there was a big sense that one phase of our lives was winding up on several fronts and a completely new era was about to begin. The time was right to switch normal life off and have a big think before switching it on again.

If you have the means to take a trip and leave your home vacant, you can always return in the unlikely event things don't work out. That wasn't an option for us. Rent from our flat was funding our adventure and we'd signed a contract to let it for a year. We had to make it work.

VANSTITUTIONALISED

One of the first big realisations that hit me was just how dependent we were on our van. I appreciate campervans and motorhomes are designed to support life on the road, but our vulnerability hit home whenever anything went wrong.

Small technical problems, which would have been a minor inconvenience on a weekend trip in the UK, feel like enormous issues when your van is your only source of transport and shelter, and you are miles from civilisation.

An amber warning light telling us to check Cliff's engine caused us immense stress on Norway's remote Lofoten islands. Our AdBlu sensor drove us to distraction in a remote mountain range. It said we'd run out of the emissions-reducing liquid, even though we'd filled up the tank earlier that day. Even worse, it warned the engine would shut down in less than fifty miles. And we knew, once an engine runs out of AdBlu it won't re-start until you add some.

What was almost worse was that both of those warnings miraculously disappeared after half a day and have never returned. And no, that wasn't good news. It made us distrust every subsequent warning message Cliff gave us.

In Albania, the smoked glass top over our sink exploded into thousands of pieces one morning after I stupidly stood a hot coffee pot on it. Not a huge issue in itself - but online research for a replacement revealed that there was no spares or any other professional support for campervans or motorhomes in the country. None at all.

Luckily, the majority of repairs on our trip were sorted with a mix of breakdown cover, a tube of sealant and a cheap tool kit from Halfords. But at the time, every problem caused much more angst that it should have done - simply because we relied on our van for everything.

During our UK stay, I confess we cheated. We spent a handful of nights in the homes of friends or relatives. Despite having very pleasant catchups, we both admitted to being strangely relieved when we settled back into the confines of our cosy, comfortable and very familiar van.

DRIVING

Steve and I have been happy to share the driving because we both love it. However, there were a few driving experiences I didn't enjoy.

We had a couple of what felt like interminable driving days heading south through Norway. It's a very long country. Long drives are the payback for enjoying the spectacular scenery in the north.

My real frustration was with the speed limits on Norway's roads - much lower than we're accustomed to in the UK. I appreciate it's for safety in a country where roads are often shrouded in mist or covered in snow. But being limited to 55 miles per hour on an all but deserted four-lane motorway when we had hundreds of miles to cover just about did my head in.

Driving in Italy wasn't the most enjoyable experience either. We thought the state of UK roads was pretty dire, but Italy's non-toll roads are in another league. We found ourselves avoiding massive potholes everywhere.

I won't fall into all the old cliches about Italian driving styles, but my drive from Rome's ring road to our campsite towards the city was an experience I will never forget. Let's leave it at that.

Albania's main roads were fine. But there aren't that many of them. Its smaller, rural roads were in a truly appalling condition - some no more than cart tracks. Having your teeth and everything else in your van rattle is quite amusing for a few minutes. When it goes on for hours, it's no fun whatsoever. Plus there's the worry that sustained driving over what feels like the surface of the Moon going to damage your van.

UNFAMILIARITY FATIGUE

We made a deliberate choice to have no detailed route plan. Our idea was to decide where we'd go and what we'd do on a daily basis. And while I have no regrets about our approach, making everything up as you go is not as carefree as it might sound. I may have discovered a new psychological phenomenon here - unfamiliarity fatigue.

Day after day of always having to think about your next move, fathoming out your route and absorbing new experiences requires mental effort.

"Pity about you!" my Mum would say. And she would be right, it is a huge privilege to have such freedom. All I'm suggesting is that you take the occasional break from continual driving and exploring.

If you find a spectacular camping spot, stay for a couple of days and re-charge your batteries. Let a small part of the world become familiar for a while and do absolutely nothing. Then you'll be refreshed for the next phase of discovery.

WEATHER WORRIES

Norwegians have a saying: "There's no such thing as bad weather - just bad clothes." Let me tell you, they are mistaken, or at least, it doesn't apply when you're living long term in a motorhome or campervan. Bad weather can have a disproportionate impact on your mood and take the shine off your adventures.

Rain, mist and low cloud conspired to deny us spectacular views on Norway's Lofoten Islands, and on the Scottish NC500. Gale-force winds almost blew us off mountains. Torrential rain confined us to the van beside a giant sand dune in Denmark and we did wake one morning in a beach-side car park to find the van surrounded by water.

Of course, we can't control the weather, just accept that it will have more of an impact on how you spend your days on a road trip than it does when you're at home.

If you're a hardy type and deliberately setting out to have an adventure in the winter snows of Northern Europe – or the Alps or Pyrenees – good on you. Just make sure you and your vehicle are fully insulated and you've packed your snow chains.

LIVING IN A BOX

It's become apparent that all our friends and relatives had been expecting the news that one of us had killed the other. To be honest, I'm a bit bored with re-assuring everyone that we really got along just fine - even though we were never more than about five metres apart in just over twelve months.

It helped that we spent at least part of each day in our own head space. Steve took time out taking and processing photos for his *Cheerfulheart Photography* project. (Check out his amazing images from our trip: https://www.instagram.com/cheerfulheartphotography).

I disappeared into writing this book, blogging on Vanlifevirgins.com and making videos for *The Campervan Channel* on YouTube.

In terms of adapting to the lack of physical space, I think we did very well. I banged my head on some part of the van every day for the first three months, but that was entirely down to clumsiness, not frustration. Rubber pads on over overhead cupboard latches and the top sill of the toilet door allowed most of my self-inflicted head injuries to heal.

I'm also a bit surprised how we survived, quite comfortably, with so little stuff. We packed nearly all our worldly belongings into our attic and my daughter's shed before we set off on our trip. We've missed none of it.

We survived perfectly well with two mugs, plates and bowls, a couple of coats, two pairs of shoes (including walking boots) and enough T-shirts and undies to last us a fortnight. Ok, I exaggerate slightly, but we jettisoned some items that we were not using en route – like the stack of eight spare towels we were convinced would be essential. We came home with much less gear than we departed with.

THE HOMECOMING

As I come to wrapping up this book, we've been home for nearly a month. It's already hard to believe that we journeyed over 21,000 miles, through twenty countries on a trip lasting one year and three weeks.

Some aspects of life are returning to the old normal. We've enjoyed catching up with friends and relatives. Steve's about to return to an NHS job and I've already picked up my old video production work.

We've re-assembled the flat but left many items in the attic because we can't work out what we ever needed them for. It's like we've been on TV's "Life Laundry" without realising it.

And shock horror - we've sold Cliff! I know. It feels like a betrayal. But he was bought specifically for our big adventure and, incredibly, we sold him for exactly what we paid for him two years ago. We've been so lucky that Post-COVID demand for leisure vehicles has kept working in our favour.

I guess the big question is would we do it all again?

We both have absolutely no regrets. And if I'd not already done it, I'd tackle a year-in-a-van adventure without hesitation. Steve is missing the travelling the lifestyle badly and is probably a candidate for permanent vanlife.

We both agree there has been only one fly in the ointment - those Schengen travel restrictions explained in Chapter Ten. If you're a Brit travelling for twelve months, the upshot is you may be forced into staying longer than you'd like in some countries - and not always at the best time of year.

In an ideal world, we should have split our adventuring into 90 day chunks and spread them over several years. But we're not retired. Work commitments and letting our flat for a year to fund our trip meant that wasn't an option for us.

But as for the overall experience, i can honestly say it has been amazing. We both appreciate that travelling in a campervan has enabled us to visit places we simply couldn't have accessed any other way. Trust us, Europe's most spectacular places don't have hotels or Airbnb's.

For us, it did take some guts, determination and resourcefulness to make our trip happen. But our nerve in trying something completely outside our comfort zone has been rewarded with hundreds of brilliant memories and experiences that we'll be processing for years.

I said at the beginning of this book that we're really not the kind of folks who do this kind of thing. Now, it seems, we are.

15. APPENDIX 1 – USEFUL APPS AND WEBSITES

Apps referred to in this appendix can usually be downloaded to your smartphone via Apple App Store of Google Play.

STOPOVER LOCATIONS

Park 4 Night - https://park4night.com/

Available via website or app. Lists thousands of official and informal camping places. Easy search for specific localities. Useful, dated reviews from previous visitors. Translates reviews instantly in all languages. Annual subscription is £6.99 Monthly subscription £1.79

Campercontact.com - https://www.campercontact.com/en

Works on web or app. Good for finding official European aires, campsites and service points. Paid for version costs €2.49 per month or €9.99 for a year. It allows app to be used offline, has more filter options, direct contacts with locations, and viewing unlimited number of sites per day. Free version has fewer features.

Camperstop.com - https://camperstop.com/en/

Details over 12,500 motorhome sites across Europe in a book, on website (free) and app (€7 euros for annual licence).

UK Motorhomes - https://www.ukmotorhomes.net/uk-stopovers/uk-stopover-listings

Online resource that lists sanctioned stopover sites for motorhomes and campervans across the UK.

All the Aires Books - https://www.vicarious-shop.com/collections/vicarious-books-media

Vicarious Media publish a range of "All the Aires" books. Detailed and frequently updated regional and country guides to official aires in Europe.

Search for Sites - https://www.searchforsites.co.uk/

Community based website and app that lists and reviews over 43,000 overnight stops and campsites. Website free. App £5.99 per year.

French Passion

Network of over 2000 French food producers who allow free 24hr stopovers in return for buying their produce. Requires current guidebook (€30 euros) which includes membership card

https://www.france-passion.com/en/motorhomers/how-it-works

Britstops - https://www.britstops.com

Book, website, and app lists over 1100 hosts at country pubs, farm shops, breweries, and other businesses that allow free overnight stays for one night. Guidebook produced annually and costs £32. Code to access app is supplied with book.

SCOTLAND

Highland Council https://www.highland.gov.uk/news/article/13790/the_highland_council_launches_welcoming_motorhome_and_camper van_guidance_for_visitors

Nature Scot
https://www.nature.scot/doc/camping-scotland

Forestry and Land Scotland
https://forestryandland.gov.scot/stay-the-night

Loch Lomond and The Trossachs National Park

General information

https://www.lochlomond-trossachs.org/th ings-to-do/camping/motorhomes-campervans-national-park/

Permit Application

https://www.lochlomond-trossachs.org/things-to-do/camping/get-a-permit/

Cairngorms National Park

Booklet

https://www.visitcairngorms.com/wp-content/uploads/2021/06/Campervan-Map-Optimised.pdf

IRELAND & NORTHERN IRELAND

Safe Nights Ireland (SNI) http://www.safenightsireland.com/ Lists over 350 safe sites for overnight stays in Ireland. Annual membership €15 if apply online.

Forestry Commission Ireland https://www.nidirect.gov.uk/services/tollymore-forest-park-camping-touring-online-booking

SPAIN - https://espana-discovery.es/

FINDING LPG

https://www.mylpg.eu/mobile/

https://www.autogas.app/

SCHENGEN ZONE RULES

Schengen Zone Countries https://www.schengenvisainfo.com/schengen-visa-countries-list/

Schengen Calculator https://ec.europa.eu/assets/home/visa-calculator/calculator.htm?lang=en

ETIAS INFORMATION AND APPLICATION

Information

https://www.schengenvisainfo.com/etias/

Application

https://www.etias.info/application/

EUROPEAN ROAD TOLLS

https://www.tolls.eu/european-countries

https://www.tollsmart.com/european-toll-calculator/

HEALTH INSURANCE

Details of NHS EIHC and GIHC Cards
https://www.nhs.uk/using-the-nhs/healthcare-abroad/apply-for-a-free-uk-global-health-insurance-card-ghic/

COVID

Up-to-date information on COVID travel restrictions

https://www.gov.uk/guidance/travel-abroad-from-england-during-coronavirus-covid-19

TRAVEL ADVICE – (ALL COUNTRIES)

Up-to-date, official travel advice from the UK Foreign Office:
https://www.gov.uk/foreign-travel-advice

DRIVING ABROAD – INSURANCE AND DRIVING LICENCE

Driving Licence Categories
https://www.gov.uk/view-driving-licence

Green card requirement (insurance)

https://www.gov.uk/vehicle-insurance/driving-abroad

International Driving Permit
https://www.gov.uk/driving-abroad/international-driving-permit

Use of winter tyres and snow chains
https://www.rac.co.uk/drive/travel/driving-in-europe/winter/

FINDING A UK PUBLIC WEIGHBRIDGE
https://www.gov.uk/find-weighbridge

ABOUT THE AUTHOR

Chris Wise

Chris Wise is a TV and video producer with a passion for anything on wheels.

After catching the campervan bug hiring a classic VW Splitty, Chris soon bought a modern Vee-Dub van and had it converted. His newbie experiences became the subject of his first book - "VW Campers for Beginners".

Then things got serious. Chris got married, put his job making videos for the NHS on hold and set off on an epic 12-month, 20,000 mile, 15-country road trip adventure in a Fiat Ducato based camper called "Cliff".

Chris is now sharing his Van Life Virgin discoveries in a series of books as well as videos for "The Campervan Channel" on YouTube

In more normal times, Chris lives in campervanning heaven - York - perfectly positioned for the North York Moors and the Yorkshire Dales.

BOOKS BY THIS AUTHOR

Vw Campers For Beginners

There's no doubt you need a VW camper. But what's the best way to turn your V-Dub desire into campervan reality?

If you're considering a ready-built camper, which iconic model makes the best buy? If you're weighing up having a Volkswagen van converted, how do you make sure you end up with the camper of your dreams? Maybe you're overwhelmed with all the options and just can't decide which route to take?

Stress not. VW Campers for Beginners is a friendly, non-nerdy guide to owning your first Volkswagen campervan. With over 80 full-colour photos, it's a helpful handbook covering topics including:

* Choosing the best VW Transporter to convert
* Picking the right converter
* Choosing campervan layouts, equipment, and accessories
* Buying air-cooled classics and modern generations
* The pros, cons and quirky features of heritage models

Inspired by the author's own experience of having his first van converted, this essential guide blends his newbie discoveries with expert advice from professional converters and campervan specialists.

It flags up the many choices you'll face when buying or converting - and offers top tips and information to help you make decisions that are right for you. Nothing too formal or techy, just useful pointers to avoid pitfalls and make your journey to owning your first VW camper as easy and exciting as is should be.

CONVERTING

If you're considering having a van converted, there's a step-by-step guide through the gazillion things you'll need to think about, including which VW Transporter models and variants make the best campers, how to find the right converter and picking the layout, seating, bed types, upholstery, essential equipment and camping accessories that will turn your dream camper into reality. It's not a detailed guide to DIY camper conversions – but seeing how the professionals do it may provide inspiration and information for folks with the skills to tackle a conversion themselves.

BUYING

If you're weighing up a ready-made campervan, there are buying guides to all six generations of Transporter and their campers. You'll discover the pros, cons and quirky characteristics of every model, from the iconic Splitties, world-beating Bay Windows and sharp-edged T3s or Vanagons; to the modern T4s, T5s and T6s.

VW CALIFORNIA

There's also a guide to the Volkswagen California – VW's highly successful in-house camper brand. Archive photos from Volkswagen Commercial Vehicles illustrate the "Cali's" development from its first incarnation on Westfalia's conversion of the VWT3 to the current family of high-end campers – including the mighty Grand Californias and the new baby- the Caddy California.

Small Dog Breeds - The Expert Guide To Finding The Best Small Dog For You

If you're searching for a small dog, but don't know which breed will suit you best, this expert guide will help you find your "pawfect" match.

You'll discover what twenty-five of our most popular small dogs are really like to live with – from hugely experienced experts who've owned their favourite type of dogs for decades.

Many of these breed gurus were recommended for this book by The Kennel Club (UK) because of their unrivalled know-how and their dedication to helping potential puppy buyers find dogs that match their lifestyles and their families.

Discover each breed's

- Temperament, quirks, and character
- Suitability with other pets and children
- Exercise and grooming demands
- Trainability – what works best with these dogs?
- Potential health issues and how to prevent them.

Their honest, no-nonsense advice allows you to narrow down your choices, comparing:

The French Bulldog, Cocker Spaniel, Miniature Dachshund, Pug, Staffordshire Bull Terrier, Miniature Schnauzer, Border Terrier, Pomeranian, Whippet, Poodle, Cavalier King Charles Spaniel, Chihuahua, Shih Tzu, Beagle, Miniature Bull Terrier, Boston Terrier, West Highland White Terrier, Lhasa Apso, Corgi, Tibetan Terrier, Shetland Sheepdog, Yorkshire Terrier, Scottish Terrier, Bichon Frise and Jack Russell Terrier.

Plus, when you've made your choice, there's expert advice on finding a reputable breeder and a step-by-step guide to the potentially tricky process of buying a puppy.

Medium And Big Dog Breeds - The Expert Guide To Finding The Best Medium-Sized Dog Or Large Dog Breed For You

If you're searching for a medium-sized or large dog, but don't know which breed will suit you best, this expert guide will help you find your "pawfect" match.

You'll discover what twenty-five of our most popular middle-sized and big dogs are really like to live with – from hugely experienced experts who've owned their favourite type of dogs for decades.

Many of these breed gurus were recommended for this book by The Kennel Club (UK) because of their unrivalled know-how and their dedication to helping potential puppy buyers find dogs that match their lifestyles and their families.

Discover each breed's
- Temperament, quirks, and character
- Suitability with other pets and children
- Exercise and grooming demands
- Trainability – what works best with these dogs?
- Potential health issues and how to prevent them.

Their honest, no-nonsense advice allows you to narrow down your choices comparing:

Medium Dogs: The Dachshund (standard), Bulldog, Springer Spaniel, Hungarian Vizsla, Standard Poodle, German Shorthaired Pointer, Bull Terrier, Border Collie, Dalmatian, Shar Pei, Siberian Husky

Large Dogs: Labrador Retriever, Golden Retriever, German Shepherd, Boxer Dog, Rottweiler, Doberman, Dogues de Bordeaux, Weimeraner, Flat-coated Retriever and Great Dane.

Plus, when you've made your choice, there's expert advice on finding a reputable breeder and a step-by-step guide to the potentially tricky process of buying a puppy.

Printed in Great Britain
by Amazon

29033008R00079